Excel In A Minute

Steps for Performing Basic Tasks in Microsoft Excel 365

Diane L. Martin

Third Edition

Excel In A Minute

Steps for Performing Basic Tasks in Microsoft Excel 365

Enhanced Third Edition

Diane L. Martin

DISCLAIMER

Copyright © 2022 Escribe Publishing. For inquiries, please email us at info@escribepublishing.com.
ISBN: 9798719511214
Library of Congress Control Number: 20211904904

Dedication

.

This book is dedicated in loving memory of my mother.
What an amazing journey Mom.

Escribe Publishing

Books for the mind, heart, and spirit

www.escribepublishing.com

Excel In A Minute

Steps for Performing Basic Tasks in Microsoft Excel 365

Third Edition

Diane L. Martin

Other Books by Diane L. Martin

The Manic Manager, How to Avoid Becoming the Manager Everybody Loves to Hate

Office In A Minute, Steps for Performing Basic Tasks in Microsoft Office 365

Office In A Minute, Steps for Performing Basic Tasks in Microsoft Office 2013

Excel In A Minute, Steps for Performing Basic Tasks in Microsoft Excel 2013

An Older Adult's Guide to the Internet & Email

Office In A Minute, Steps for Performing Basic Tasks in Microsoft Excel 2013

Windows In A Minute, Steps for Performing Basic Tasks in Microsoft Windows 8.1

Between The World and Me, When Three Voices Speak As One

Editorial Notes:

Chapter Timings

 Timings are designed to provide the reader with an estimate of the time necessary to complete the tasks within each chapter. Be advised that some readers may find that they can complete the tasks in less time, while others may require more time based on their experience and level of computer proficiency. The timings should be considered a guide, and do not represent a guarantee of a reader's performance.

More to Learn

This symbol means there is more to this feature than covered in the section. Additional menus, options, or dialog boxes are available.

Truncated Ribbons

Whenever possible we strive to depict all of the commands available on a particular screen. However, please be advised that a truncated view may be displayed due to space limitations.

Left-Click/Right-Click

Mouse click instructions assume that most users are right-handed. This includes references to left and right mouse clicks. Mouse orientation may be changed in the Windows Control Panel.

Microsoft OneDrive

References are made throughout the text to Microsoft OneDrive. OneDrive is an application that permits users to store documents in the cloud so that they are essentially accessible anywhere there is an Internet connection. OneDrive was formerly known as SkyDrive. For more information about how you can sign-up for OneDrive, visit www.microsoft.com.

.

Table of Contents

When You Need to Learn Fast

Includes coverage of Word, Excel, Outlook, PowerPoint, and OneNote

Be more productive at home, at work or in school

Available at Amazon.com and other online book retailers

Short Table of Contents

About This Book

The purpose of this book is to serve as a quick tutorial for anyone eager to learn the features, functions, and benefits of Microsoft Excel. If you want to learn the most salient features of this very robust application, you have come to the right place. Included, as a bonus is coverage of several advanced features like Pivot Tables, Conditional Formatting, and the VLOOKUP functions to name a few. Chapter timings are designed to give you an idea of just how long it should take you to complete the tasks included. Additionally, there are practice exercises (located in the Appendix) as well as handy note pages included throughout the book.

Through this handy tutorial you will learn how to:

- Open an Existing Worksheet
- Insert a new worksheet
- Edit an existing worksheet
- Use the SUM, AVERAGE, MIN, MAX, NOW, TODAY, VLOOKUP, and IF functions
- Work with the COUNT functions
- Distinguish Between Clearing and Deleting the Contents of a Cell
- Save a Workbook
- Quickly calculate data with the AutoSum Feature
- Use the Fill Series Feature
- Create Named Ranges
- Print a Worksheet
- Use the Spelling Feature
- Format Cells Using Bold, Underline, or Italics
- Insert a Charts, Dashboards, and Sparklines into a Worksheet
- Work with Templates
- Create Pivot Tables and Charts
- Apply Conditional Formatting
- Analyze Data by Creating Tables and much, much more.

The wonderful thing about Excel is that most features and functions are capable of being performed in two minutes or less. Practice using them regularly, and before you know it, you will begin to recall them effortlessly.

For solutions to our practice exercises, email us at learner@escribepublishing.com

Finally, note that reference is made throughout this document to Excel or MS-Excel; both are references to the Microsoft Excel spreadsheet application.

Happy Computing!

Microsoft Excel

"Pure mathematics is, in its way, the poetry of logical ideas."

~ Albert Einstein

Chapter 1

GETTING STARTED WITH EXCEL

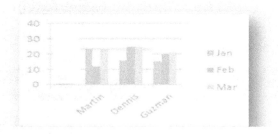

- **Start the Excel Application**

- **Structure and Enter Data**

- **Work with Basic Formulas**

- **Use the AutoSum Feature**

- **Save a Workbook**

- **Close a Workbook**

The Estimated Time to Complete These Tasks is 25 –30 Minutes.

Starting the Microsoft Excel Application

Microsoft Excel is an application designed to facilitate the management of numerical data. This means that Excel can be used for everything from managing a household budget to forecasting and calculating sales for a major corporation.

Start the Excel Application from your desktop by clicking on the Microsoft Excel icon. Excel opens to a single electronic worksheet. A worksheet is made up of addressable cells, rows, and columns. A cell is the intersection of a row and a column. With 16,384 columns and 1,048,576 rows per worksheet, you will have plenty of space. Observe that when you click your mouse into a cell, it becomes the "active cell". Note the status bar at the bottom of Figure 1. The word "Ready" indicates that you may edit or perform some other tasks within the worksheet.

If you do need more worksheets, adding them to your workbook is a cinch. Simply click on the Add Worksheet button located at the bottom of your workbook.

The Microsoft Excel Environment

Figure 1

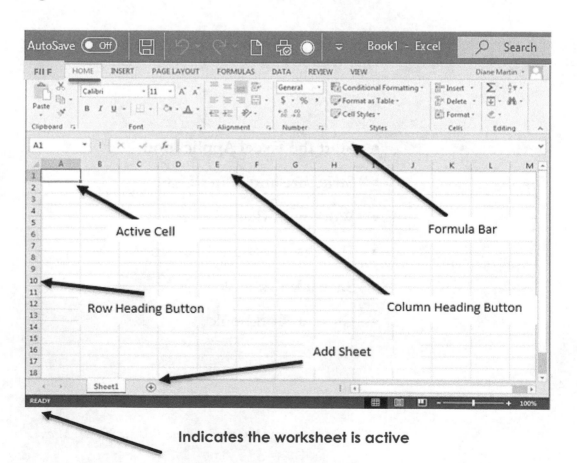

Microsoft Excel Ribbons and Tabs

Examine the tabs at the top of the Excel window. Each tab contains a ribbon with features organized around frequently used commands. For example, notice the Font group includes the Bold, *Italics,* and <u>Underline</u> buttons.

Since a cell is the intersection of a row and a column, it has an address. Look at the image below and notice the address of the highlighted or active cell is D10. This address also appears in the Name box. Once again examine Figure 2. Referring to cells by address makes it easier to change and calculate the content within those cells.

Cells may contain text, numbers, or formulas. While we cover formulas in a little more detail later; keep in mind that a formula differs from text. When entering a formula, you must always begin with an equal (=) symbol.

Figure 2

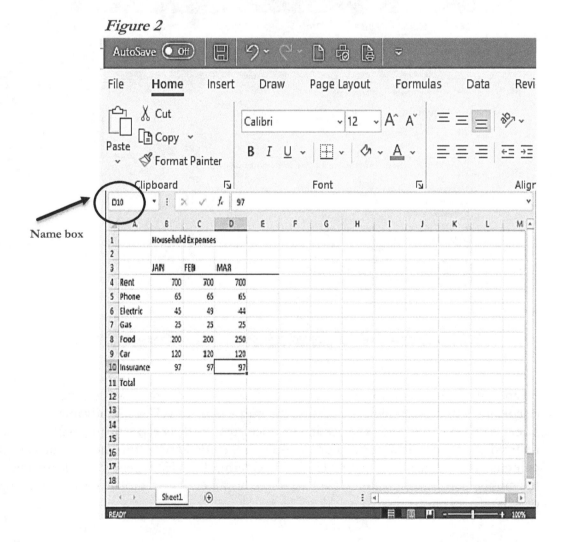

Name box

Structuring and Entering Worksheet Data

Creating a worksheet is a little like using numbers to tell a story. For example, notice in Figure 3, that my worksheet has a title. This is the introduction to my worksheet. This simple structure communicates the purpose of the worksheet and includes the date it was created. Now others will understand what my worksheet is all about. For practice, try creating the worksheet depicted in Figure 3.

To enter data into your worksheet, simply click your mouse in the cell where you want to begin typing. If you type a number or letter into a cell and then change your mind, click on the Cancel (☒) button depicted in the figure below. Click on the Accept (☑) or Enter key to confirm your entry.

Figure 3

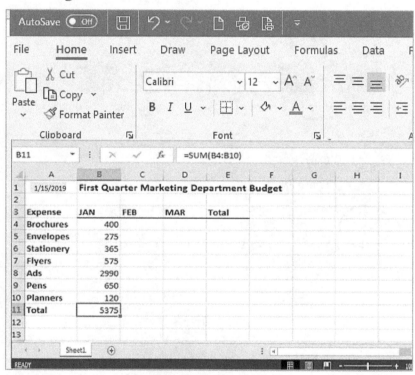

I can use a calculator to add the contents of the January data; however, manually calculating this way would really defeat the purpose of Excel. A key advantage of using Excel is that it can quickly and accurately calculate as well as allow us to perform what is referred to as what-if analysis. For example, if we construct a formula to calculate the contents of the cells B5 through B13, (in Excel terms: B5:B13) we can go back and change the numbers in any cell within that range to see how it effects our total. That is an example of what-if analysis.

SUM, AVERAGE, MIN, MAX, NOW, and TODAY

Excel's built-in formulas allow you to calculate any range of numbers quickly. Remember that all formulas must be preceded by an equal (=) sign. This is how Excel distinguishes between what can and cannot be calculated. To add a range of numbers, such as the one depicted in Figure 4, you would click into cell B11 and type the following: **=SUM(B4:10)**. The argument is contained within the parenthesis.

Some Basic Functions in Microsoft Excel

1. Click your mouse in the cell where you want the result to appear.

2. Type an = and then type the desired formula.

3. To add a range of numbers use **= SUM(B4:B10)**

4. To calculate the average for a range use **=AVERAGE(B4:B10)**

5. To display the lowest number in a range use **=MIN(B4:B10)**

6. To display the highest number in a range use **= MAX (B4:B10)**

7. To display the current date and time use **= NOW() or =TODAY()**

The AutoSum Feature

You can rapidly add up any range of numbers using the Home Tab's AutoSum button. Think of AutoSum as a shortcut that eliminates the need to type out an entire formula, i.e., **=SUM (B4:B10)** See the figure below.

To Use the AutoSum Feature

1. Select the Home tab.

2. Place your cursor in the result cell.

3. Click on the AutoSum button. (*Notice the other AutoSum functions*, i.e., MAX)

4. Press the enter key to accept the selected range.

Note: The functions **NOW** and **TODAY** do not use arguments.

Figure 4

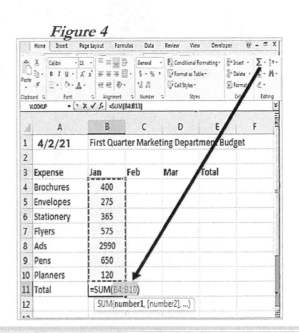

Saving A Workbook

While the Excel application is open, your worksheet exists in your computer's memory. Memory is volatile and is easily disrupted by a power fluctuation or outage. Therefore, until your worksheet is saved to some permanent media like a hard drive, flash drive, or your Microsoft OneDrive, you risk its complete loss. For this reason, make it a practice to save your workbook at regular intervals. The first time you choose the Save menu option, The Save As window will open. At this point, you must give your workbook a name.

To Save a Workbook

1. Click on the File tab, and then choose the Save menu option.

2. Click on the Browse button to choose a location for your workbook.

3. When prompted type a name for your workbook.

4. Click on the Save button.

Figure 5

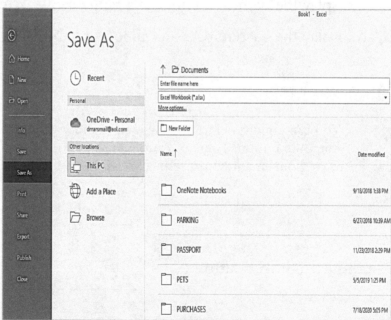

Opening and Closing an Existing Workbook

If you want to close your workbook, but remain in Excel, simply click on the File tab, and then select the Close menu option. To open a new workbook, simply click on the File tab and then select Open from the menu. You can have any number of opened workbooks. The maximum limit is a factor of your computer memory and system resources. However, to minimize confusion, you will want to avoid keeping multiple workbooks open at the same time.

My Notes:

My Notes:

Chapter 2

MANAGING PAGE SETUP
&
PRINTING OPTIONS

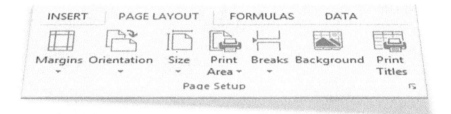

- Print a Workbook

- Identify Page Layout Options

- Work with the Page Setup Feature

- Set the Worksheet Print Area

 The Estimated Time to Complete These Tasks is 7.5 Minutes.

Printing in Microsoft Excel

One of the best things about Excel is that there are several ways to initiate printing. For example, you can select the Print option from the File tab, or you can initiate printing using the Quick Access toolbar. Alternatively, you can also access the Print command by choosing the Page Layout tab, and then selecting the Page Setup drop-down box.

As you become more familiar with Excel, you can experiment with the various options, and then select the method you like the best. Since ribbons and tabs are so convenient, this is the method we will cover in detail here.

When you select the Print menu option from the File tab's Backstage view, you will see that Excel displays a facsimile of what the worksheet will look like in hard copy. Notice that the worksheet displays gridlines. In addition, there is neither a header nor footer in this worksheet. The printing of these kinds of elements can be accomplished through Excel's Page Setup options.

Printing a Worksheet

1. Click on the File tab.

2. Choose the Print menu option.

3. Click on the Print button.

Figure 6

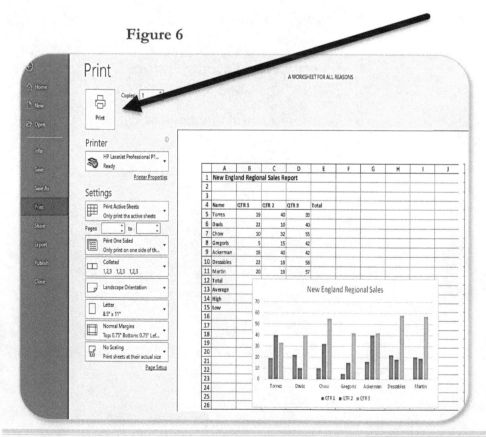

Page Setup Options

Excel makes it possible to manage the layout of your worksheet with a wide variety of options. For example, you can insert headers and footers into your worksheet. In addition, you can choose to display and print out your worksheet in the landscape as opposed to portrait orientation. The row and column headers as well as the gridlines you view on the screen may also be printed in Excel.

You access Page Setup options from the Page Layout tab. See Figure 7 and notice the tiny drop-down box within the Page Setup group. When you click on this drop-down box, the Page Setup dialog box opens and displays several tabs: Page, Margins, Header/Footer, and Sheet. In addition, if you click on the Print Preview button, you can see what your worksheet will look like when printed. See the next page for a description of Excel's Page Setup options.

Figure 7

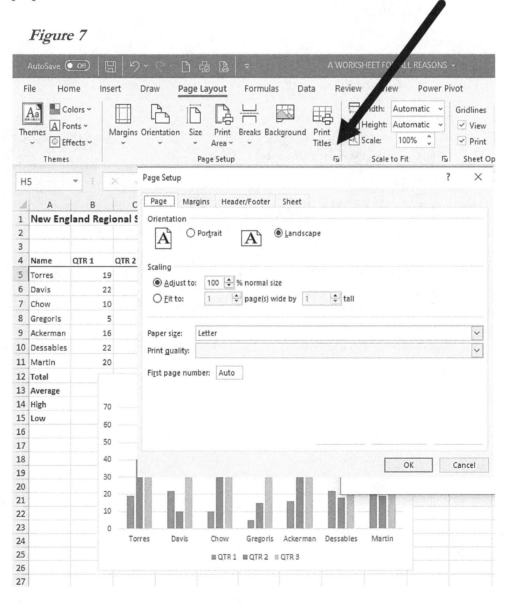

Adjusting Page Settings

From the Page tab, you can change the orientation of your worksheet from Portrait to landscape. In addition, because worksheets can grow to become quite large, they do not always print out as planned. Therefore, Excel allows you to adjust the size of your worksheet through its many scaling options. See Figure 8 below.

You may want to use the Fit to option when you are working with a particularly large worksheet, and it must fit on a single worksheet. Worksheets that span multiple pages can be difficult to manage so Fit to can be very useful. One caveat, however, is that this feature can cause Excel to reduce the size of your font making it difficult to read. For this reason, you may prefer using the Adjust to option. Simply click on the spin box to decrease or increase scaling.

Figure 8

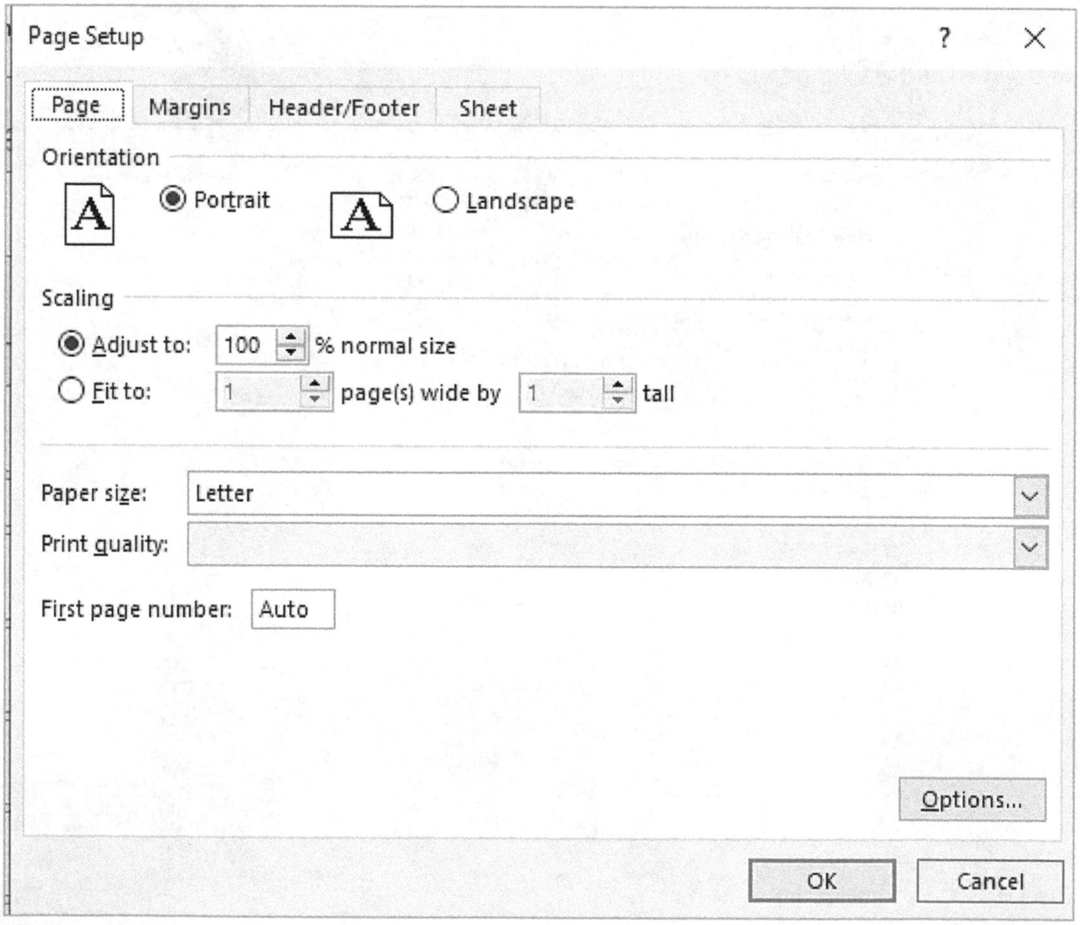

Setting Margins in Excel

One of the ways you can control the appearance of your worksheets is by adjusting margin settings through the Page Layout dialog box. From the Margins tabs, you can modify default settings for not only left and right margins but for your headers and footers as well. Simply click on the adjacent spin boxes to select the desired parameters. See Figure 9. As you make your adjustments notice the worksheet facsimile changes to approximate how your worksheet will appear. Choose OK to save your modifications. If you select the Options button Excel will display adjustable printer properties for the default printer.

Figure 9

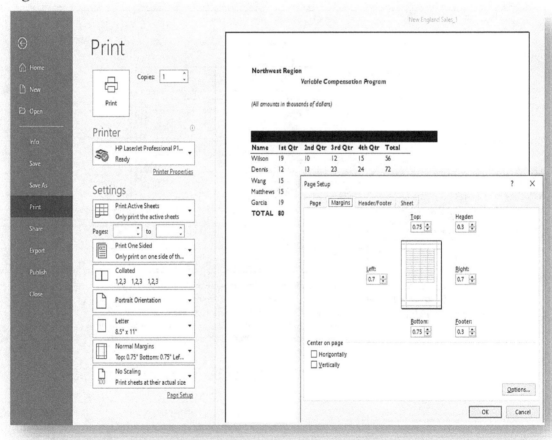

Headers and Footers

A header is a section within the top margin of a document or in this case, a worksheet. A footer likewise is a section that appears within the bottom margin of your worksheet. Both headers and footers can be used to organize your worksheet. For example, a header might contain the word draft, or it may include your department or company name. Alternatively, you might use a footer to include the date and/or the location of your file.

Select the Header/Footer tab to choose from a list of built-in headers and footers or design your own by choosing the Custom Header or Custom Footer buttons. Your headers or footers can include pictures, the date, and/or the name of your file. See Figure 10 below. Headers and footers can also contain up to 255 characters.

Figure 10

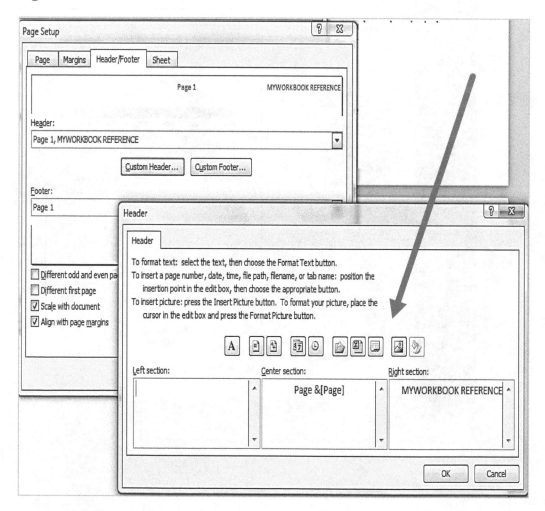

Basic Sheet Tab Controls

From the Sheet tab, you can elect to print for example the gridlines in your worksheet. In addition, you can elect to print the familiar row and column headings that appear on the screen. See Figure 11 below and note both the gridlines and row and column headers checkboxes. Additionally, note the Print area field. This is yet another way to limit what you print to a specific range in your worksheet. This is a particularly useful feature if you are working with a large worksheet. The adjacent dropdown box can be used to highlight the rows you want to be repeated when there is a page break in your worksheet.

Through Excel, you can also add comments and notes to a cell. By default, those comments will not print; however, you can prompt Excel to print them by selecting the comments and notes dropdown box.

Figure 11

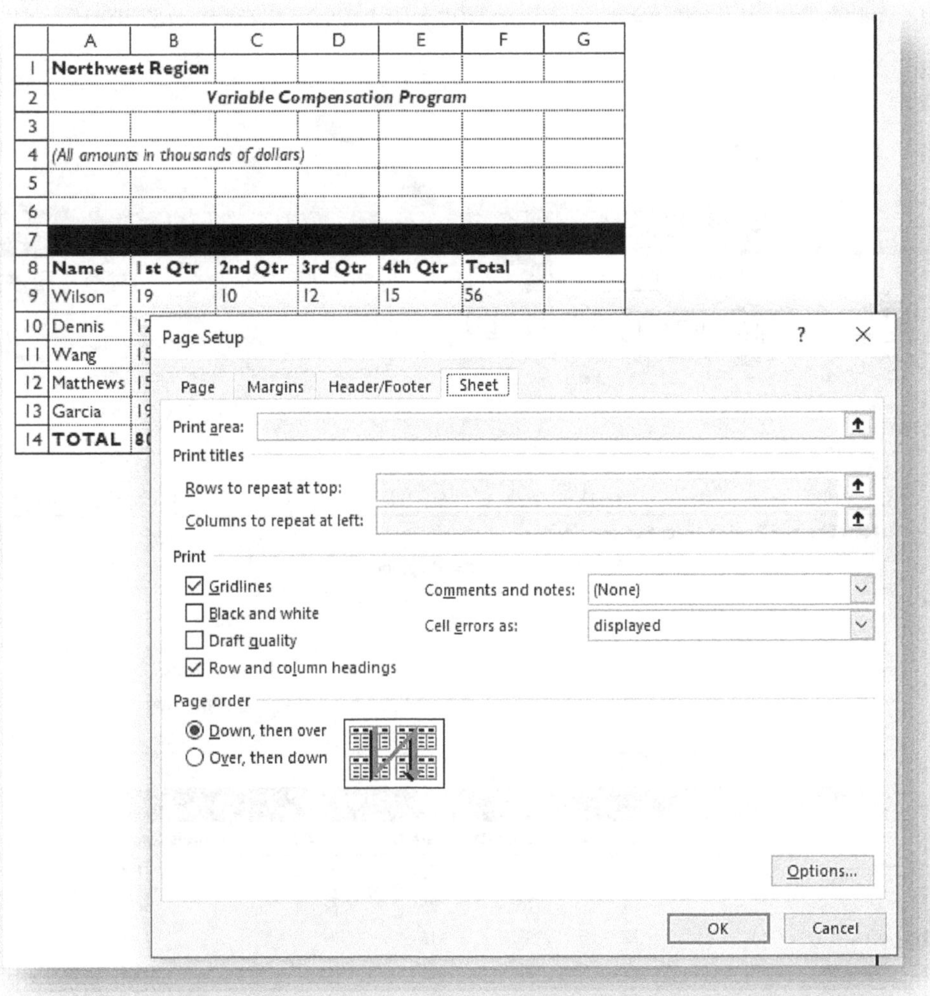

Controlling the Worksheet Print Area

Worksheets can become rather extensive, and thus, the ability to isolate and print a specific section of a worksheet is a real advantage. Excel's Set Print Area feature is located within the Page Setup group. See Figure 12 below and note that the range selected includes only B8:D13.

Setting the Print Area

1. Drag your mouse to select the range of data to be printed.

2. Click on the Page Layout tab.

3. Click on the Print Area drop-down box.

4. Choose the Set Print Area menu option.

5. Click on the File tab and choose the Print menu option to print the area.

Figure 12

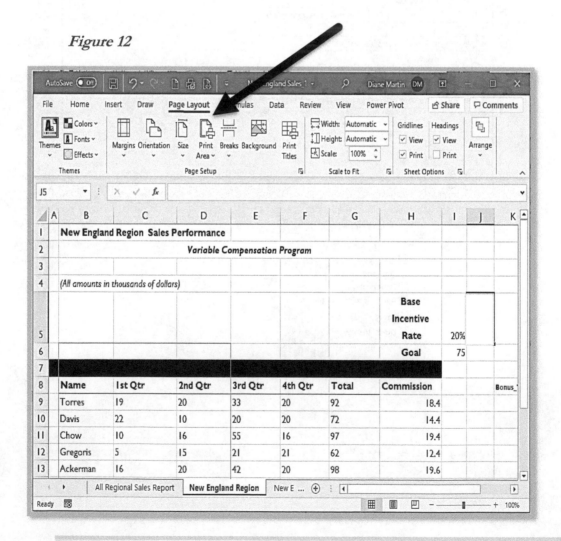

A Worksheet After Setting the Print Area

After selecting Print from the File tab, Excel displays a facsimile of your worksheet. See Figure 13. The display is properly limited to the selected range. Refer to Figure 12. Here you can also view other print options. Notice too that Portrait orientation is the default print option. Alternatively, you can select Landscape Orientation from the same dropdown box.

Figure 13

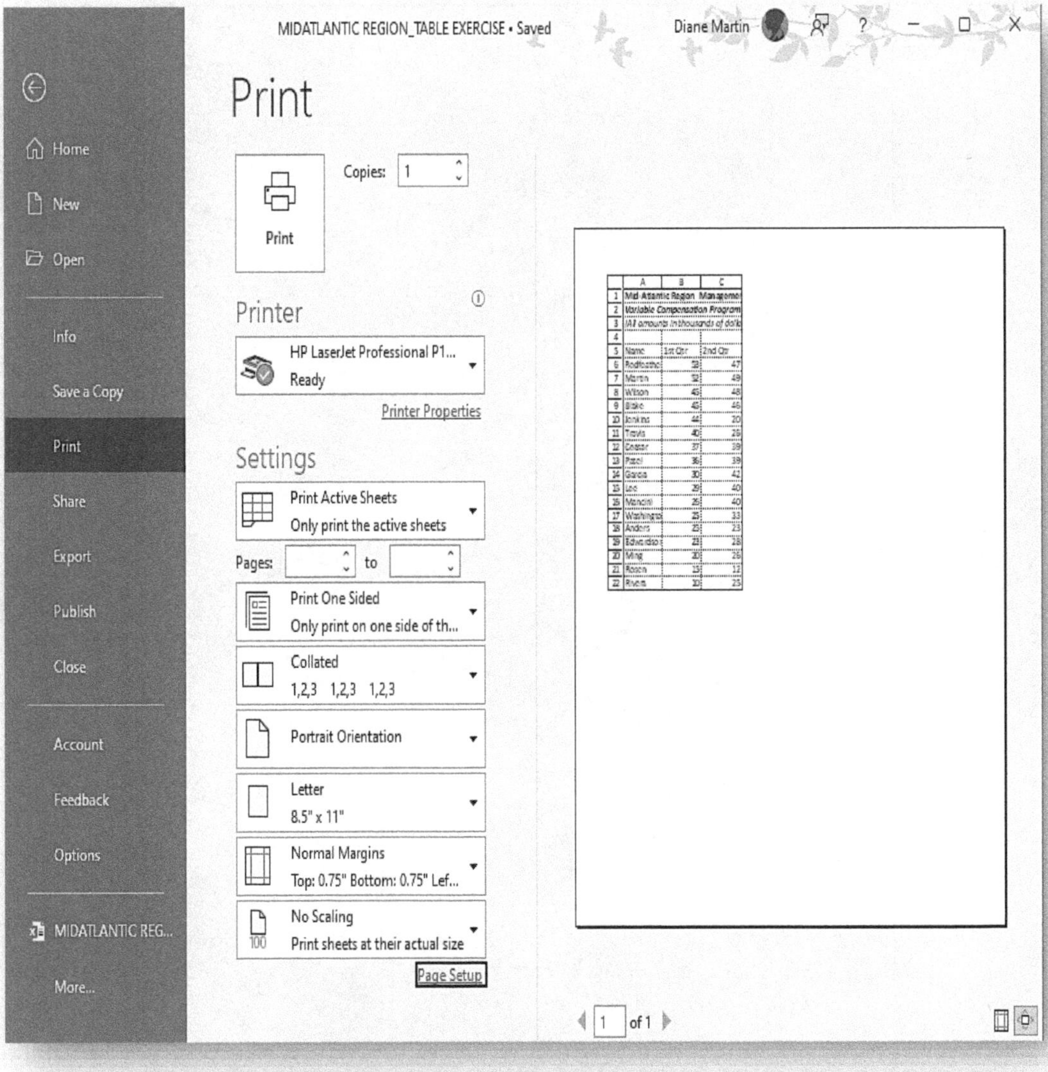

My Notes:

Chapter 3

MANAGING

&

FORMATTING WORKSHEETS

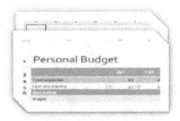

- **Format Cells**

- **Clear or Delete Cell Contents**

- **Insert Rows and Columns**

- **Apply Character Formatting**

- **Use Alignment group Buttons**

- **Use the Format Painter Feature**

- **Undo your Last Command**

- **Use the Spelling Feature**

- **Copy Formulas**

- **Create Relative and Absolute Cell References**

 The Estimated Time to Complete These Tasks is 15 Minutes.

Formatting Cells

You will be pleased to learn that Excel makes formatting cells very straightforward. Both text and numerical data may be formatted to include dollar signs, percentage symbols, decimals, and commas. For example, if you want to represent financial data, you will find the Number group on the Home tab quite useful. Simply select the cell you wish to format, and then click on the Currency Style button. Note that some of the available formatting options include the Comma and Percentage styles. See Figure 14.

Alternatively, you can click on the Number group drop-down box; and then select from a wide array of formatting options. See the dialog box depicted in Figure 14-A. It has been said that there are at least three different ways to perform most tasks in Microsoft Office, and options for formatting cells are just one example of how versatile Excel can be. Another way to format selected cells is by clicking on the General dropdown box. Notice how many cell formatting options are available. Remember to first select the data you want to format.

Figure 14

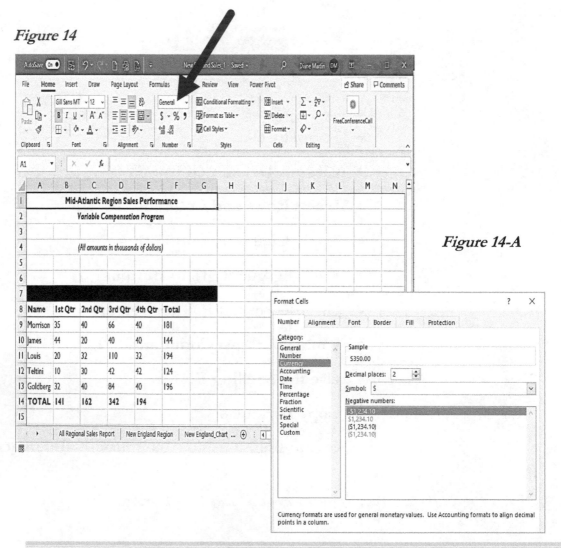

Figure 14-A

Clearing or Deleting the Contents of a Cell

Inevitably, you will need to delete some or all the information you have typed into your worksheet. Fortunately, Excel has a button for that. You can choose to either clear the contents of a cell or delete the contents. See the Figure 15 below. Note that if I click into cell D4 for example and press the right mouse button, a short menu is displayed.

The distinction between Delete and Clear Contents is an important one. When you choose the Clear Contents menu option, any formatting within the cell, i.e., currency symbol or percentage will remain. On the other hand, if you choose the Delete option, the formatting will be deleted along with the data within the cell.

To Clear or Delete the Contents of a Cell

1. Select the cell(s) to be cleared or deleted.

2. Right-click your mouse and choose the Clear Contents or Delete.

Figure 15

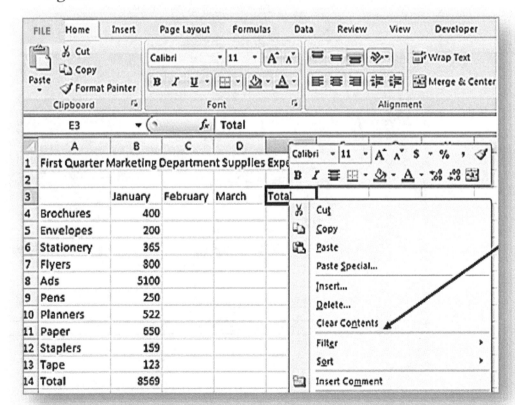

Managing the Worksheet

Additional cells, rows, and/or columns are added to a worksheet by using buttons located on the Home tab. Examine the Cells group and you will find the Insert and Delete Cells menu options. Now see Figure 16 and notice the row has been selected by clicking on the row-heading button. You can follow the same process for columns.

To Insert Rows and Columns

1. Click on the desired row or column-heading button.

2. Click on the Home tab.

3. Click on the Insert drop-down box within the Cells group.

4. Select the Insert Sheet Rows button.

5. Repeat the steps above for deleting rows and columns.

To Insert a Worksheet

1. Click on the Insert drop-down box
   Choose the Insert Sheet menu option.

Figure 16

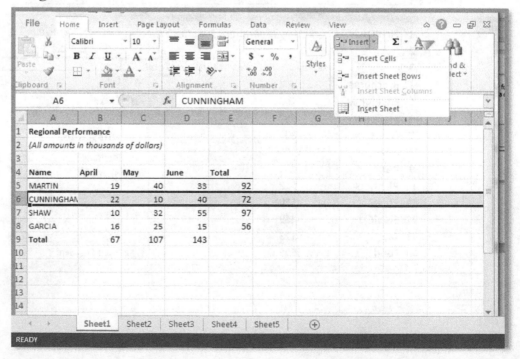

Apply Character Formatting

You can focus your reader's attention by applying Microsoft Excel's text formatting features within your worksheet. With one keystroke and in less than three seconds, you can bold, underline, italicize, color, or change the typeface within a worksheet.

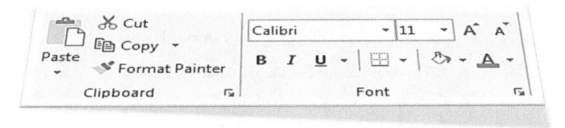

To Apply Bold, *Italicized*, or <u>Underline</u> Formatting

1. Drag or click your mouse to select the cell to be formatted.
2. Click on the desired formatting button, i.e., B, *I,* or <u>U</u>

To Apply a New Font

Try changing the current font in your worksheet to Calibri.

1. Select the cell to be changed.
2. Click on the Font drop-down box and choose the Calibri font.
3. Click on the Font Size button if you want to change the size of the text.

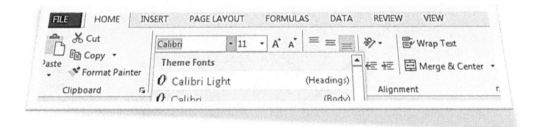

Alignment Group Buttons

Align text or numerical data within your cells by using the Alignment group buttons: Left, Center, Right, and Justify. Remember to first select the cell, and then click on the desired alignment button.

Formatting Data with Excel

Good News! If you have ever worked with Microsoft Word, then you already know what a time-saver the Format Painter can be. This feature in Excel allows you to copy the character formatting of a cell and then apply it to the contents of another cell.

To Use the Format Painter

1. Click on the cell that contains the desired formatting.

2. Click on the Format Painter to copy the formatting.

3. Select the target cell to apply the formatting.

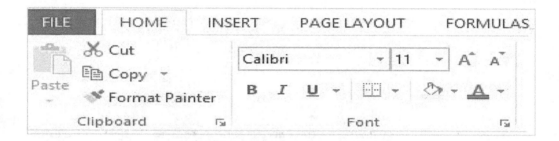

Clear Formatting

If you change your mind and wish to remove any formatting you have applied, simply click on the clear formatting drop-down button. This will erase any formatting such as bold or underline from the selected text.

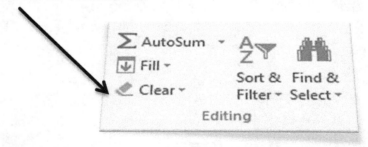

Undo Your Last Command

You can also undo your last keystrokes by clicking on Microsoft's wonderful and multi-level Undo button. Excel actually has 100 undo levels. You can find this button located on the Quick Access Toolbar.

Mind Your Spelling

Microsoft Excel contains a spelling-checking feature that will automatically check your workbook for common spelling and grammatical errors. Note that proper nouns and words typed in all capitals are generally not picked up by the Spelling feature.

1. Click on the Review tab.

2. Click on the Spelling button.

3. To accept a suggested correction, click the Change button.

Figure 17

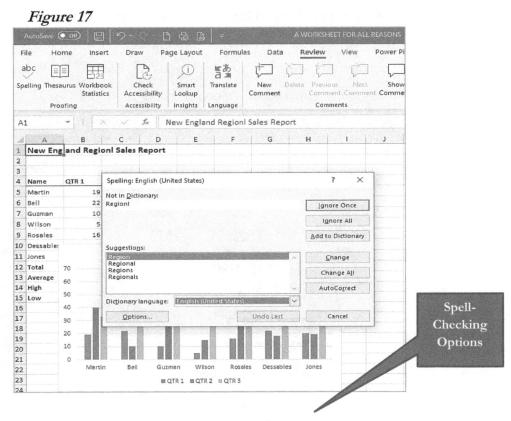

- <u>Ignore Once</u>: Prompts Excel to skip a word that is not in the dictionary.

- <u>Add to Dictionary:</u> Adds the selected word to your customized dictionary so the word will not be flagged again.

- <u>Ignore All</u>: Prompts Excel to ignore all occurrences of a word not in its dictionary.

- <u>AutoCorrect:</u> Prompts Excel to check its AutoCorrect entries for the correct spelling of a word.

- <u>Change:</u> Substitutes the flagged word for a suggested correction.

- <u>Change All:</u> Universal substitution of the flagged word for the suggested word.

Managing Data with Cut, Copy and Paste

There will be times when you will want to copy data from one cell to another. Alternatively, you may need to permanently move data from one cell to another. Excel has a Cut, Copy and Paste feature that allows you to do this in mere seconds. There are several ways to copy or move data within Excel. You will find these features conveniently located within the Clipboard group of the Home tab.

To Copy the Contents of a Cell

1. Select the Home tab.

2. Click your mouse into the cell you want to copy.

3. Click your right mouse button and then choose Copy.

4. Click your mouse on the target cell, and then click on the Paste button.

5. Press the Esc key (to halt the copy process).

Figure 18

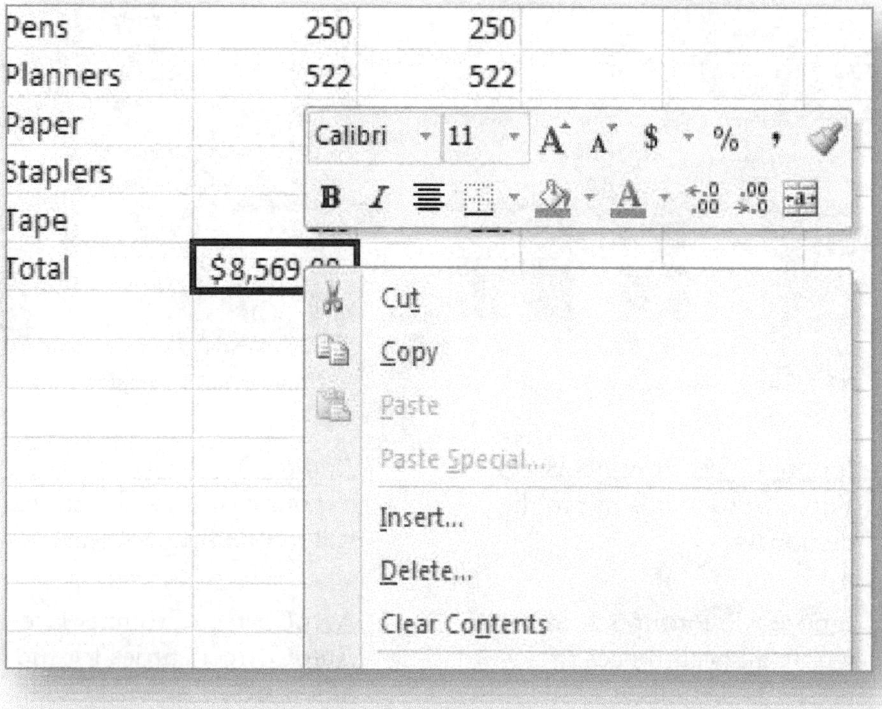

Short-Cut Keys

Try using these Microsoft Office short-cut keystrokes. They are an alternative for selecting the cut, copy and paste buttons from the Excel Clipboard Group. It's still true that whatever you copy is moved temporarily to Excel's Clipboard. Just select the data, choose copy, and then place your cursor where you want to paste it. Press Ctrl + V and it is done! Use Ctrl + X to cut text.

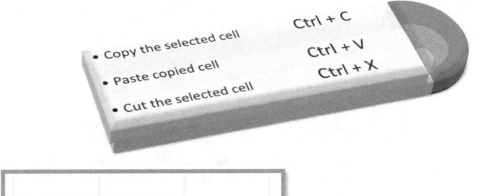

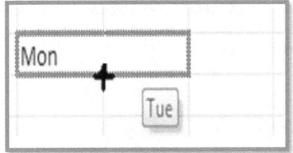

The Fill Series Feature

Microsoft Excel also has a wonderful feature known as the Fill Handle. Once you have mastered using this timesaving method, you will become hooked, and you will forever look for ways to put it to work for you. The Fill Handle can be used to fill a series of cells. For example, suppose you want your worksheet to list the days of the week. You could type the days of the week into each of seven cells, or you could type the word Monday and then drag your mouse across six columns and have Excel populate the cells for you.

Use the Fill Handle to Create a Series

1. Type the first word of the series, i.e., Monday.

2. Move your mouse over the lower right corner of a cell; see the crosshair.

3. Drag your mouse across the number of cells in the series.

Excel comes with several pre-set series like the days of the week and months of the year, but you can also create your own series through the Options menu.

Copying Formulas

The Fill Handle may be used to copy formulas from one cell to another. For example, suppose you want to copy the formula in cell B:14 to cell C:14. Hover with your mouse over the lower right corner of the cell you want to copy; when the fill handle (+) appears, drag your mouse to the adjacent cell. Alternatively, you can use the Copy and Paste buttons located on the Home tab.

When a formula is copied, its cell address changes relative to its new location. This is what is referred to as a relative cell reference. Look at Figure 19 below and notice the formula in C14 is =SUM (C9:C13). When copied to column D the formula becomes =SUM (D9:D13). Generally, this is the result you want; however, there will be times when you do not want a formula to change when copied.

Relative Versus Absolute References

Making a cell reference absolute is not difficult. All you need to do is place a dollar sign before the row and column. For example, $I$5 is an example of an absolute cell reference. You can expect to find these references in more complex worksheets. See the next page for more about how absolute references work.

Figure 19

	A	B	C	D	E	F	G	H	I
1			New England Region Sales Performance						
2			Variable Compensation Program						
3									
4			(All amounts in thousands of dollars)						
5								Base Incentive Rate	0.2
6								Goal	75
7									
8		Name	1st Qtr	2nd Qtr	3rd Qtr	4th Qtr	Total	Commission	
9		Torres	19	20	33	20	=SUM(C9:F9)	=G9*$I$5	
10		Davis	22	10	20	20	=SUM(C10:F10)	=G10*$I$5	
11		Chow	10	16	55	16	=SUM(C11:F11)	=G11*$I$5	
12		Gregoris	5	15	21	21	=SUM(C12:F12)	=G12*$I$5	
13		Ackerman	16	20	42	20	=SUM(C13:F13)	=G13*$I$5	
14		TOTAL	=SUM(C9:C13)	=SUM(D9:D13)	=SUM(E9:E13)	=SUM(F9:F13)			
15									

An Absolute Reference At Work

Examine the worksheet in Figure 20 below, and notice the formula used to calculate the sales tax for items within the store inventory. The use of the absolute reference $E$2 is required to ensure that when the Fill handle is used to copy the formula in cell E2 down, Excel multiplies the tax by the total for each product.

Without the absolute reference $E$2 Excel would do the following: (B4*C4)*E2, then (B5*C5)*E3 then (B6*C6)*E4. Obviously, this would not be a desirable result. This is the reason absolute references are necessary.

You can view the formulas within a worksheet by clicking on the Show Formulas button located within the Formula Auditing ribbon. Again see the lower half of Figure 20 below to examine what the worksheet looks like when the Show Formulas button is selected. In addition, you can use the FORMULATEXT function to display the content of a specific cell. For example, click into cell G2 and type =FORMULATEXT(E11) to display the formula in that cell.

To become a little more comfortable with absolute references, try recreating my worksheet below.

Figure 20

A Formula with an absolute reference.

	A	B	C	D	E	F	G	H
1	Store Inventory							
2	Sales Tax				6.5%			
3	Item	Price	Quanity	Sales Tax	Total			
4	Pens	3.99	10	2.59	42.49			
5	Pencils	2.99	12	2.33	38.21			
6	Erasers	1.79	16	1.86	30.50			
7	Staplers	4.99	25	8.11	132.86			
8	Note Pads	6.79	30	13.24	216.94			
9	Tape	3.29	19	4.06	66.57			
10	Calculators	5.98	20	7.77	127.37			
11	Total		132	39.97	654.95			
12								
13	Store Inventory							
14	Sales Tax					0.065		
15	Item	Price	Quanity	Sales Tax		Total		
16	Pens	3.99	10	=(B4*C4)*$E$2		=(B4*C4)+D4	The Show
17	Pencils	2.99	12	=(B5*C5)*$E$2		=(B5*C5)+D5	Formula
18	Erasers	1.79	16	=(B6*C6)*$E$2		=(B6*C6)+D6	View
19	Staplers	4.99	25	=(B7*C7)*$E$2		=(B7*C7)+D7	
20	Note Pads	6.79	30	=(B8*C8)*$E$2		=(B8*C8)+D8	
21	Tape	3.29	19	=(B9*C9)*$E$2		=(B9*C9)+D9	
22	Calculators	5.98	20	=(B10*C10)*$E$2		=(B10*C10)+D10	
23	Total		=SUM(C4:C10)	=SUM(D4:D10)		=SUM(E4:E10)	

My Notes:

Chapter 4

Enhancing Worksheets With Images and Objects

- **Place Illustrations within a Worksheet**

- **Insert Hyperlinks into a Worksheet**

- **Use the SmartArt Feature**

- **Enhance a Worksheet with Shapes**

- **Save Time with Templates**

- **Work with Drawing Tools**

 The Estimated Time to Complete These Tasks is 21 Minutes.

Inserting Illustrations

Excel makes the placement of illustrations, photographs, or stock images within a worksheet very simple to do. Keep in mind that your pictures are generally stored in your My Pictures Library, so if the picture you need is there, choose This Device from the Insert Picture menu. However, to access Microsoft's online Pictures gallery, choose Online Pictures. See Figure 21.

Note that in addition to Online Pictures, Microsoft provides a portal for third-party stock images. You can explore these images by selecting Stock Images from the Insert Picture menu.

1. Click on the Insert tab.

2. Choose a source for your images.

3. Type the name of the desired object in the Search field.

5. Click on the desired image.

6. Click on the Insert button.

Figure 21

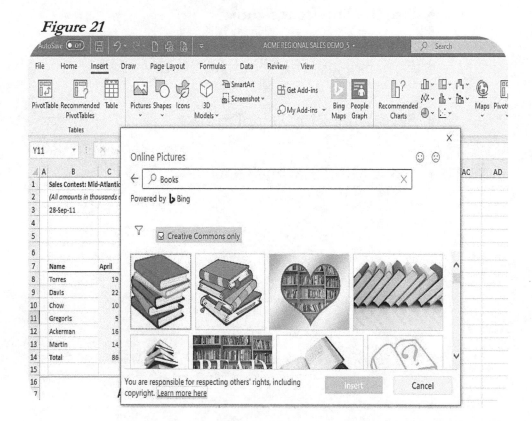

Sizing or Adjusting Images

After you select your image, Excel places it into your worksheet surrounded by handles. See Figure 22 below.

To make the image larger or smaller, simply hover with your mouse over any of the handles and notice the double arrow. When the double arrow appears, hold down your left mouse button and drag it left or right to size the image.

Figure 22

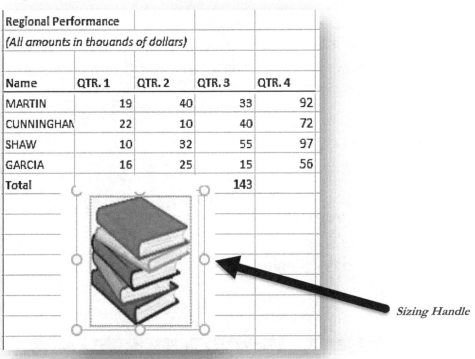

Regional Performance				
(All amounts in thouands of dollars)				
Name	QTR. 1	QTR. 2	QTR. 3	QTR. 4
MARTIN	19	40	33	92
CUNNINGHAN	22	10	40	72
SHAW	10	32	55	97
GARCIA	16	25	15	56
Total			143	

Sizing Handle

If you do not have much experience working with Word's graphic images, you may find it a bit intimidating at first. But worry not; practice makes perfect. In no time at all, you will find the manipulation of pictures both fun and gratifying. The key is to just relax. It is all a matter of pointing, clicking, and dragging the object. Remember, to size a graphic image, you must first select the image and then drag your mouse towards or away from you to size it.

To delete an image, simply select the image and then press the delete key. Remember, that if you accidentally delete an image, you can restore it by clicking the Undo button.

Insert Links into a Worksheet

The ability to work with multiple worksheets simultaneously is a real advantage in Microsoft Excel. For this reason, you will come to appreciate the Links feature. This feature enables you to insert a hyperlink into your worksheet. Essentially you can create an electronic link from one location within a worksheet to another location, i.e., a worksheet, cell, or an existing Excel file on your computer. Examine Figure 23 below and you will notice that it contains several worksheets. I have placed a link into my New England Region worksheet that when selected, takes the user to the worksheet named Southeast Region. For a particularly large workbook, this is really helpful.

Moreover, you can also include links to websites or other external documents. Excel 365 recognizes an Internet address when entered into a cell and will automatically convert it to a hyperlink. Thus, if you enter www.microsoft.com, the hyperlink will appear as soon as you press the Enter key. Additionally, a hyperlink can be represented by text or an image. See the next page for instructions on how to insert a link into your Excel worksheet.

Figure 23

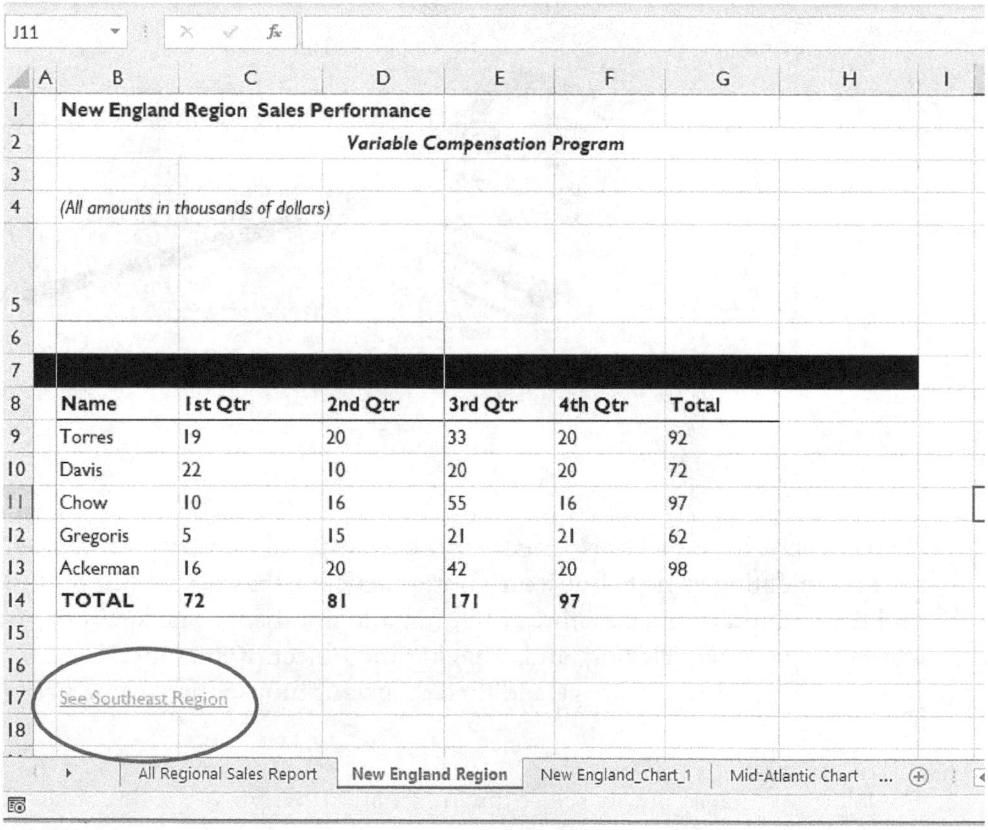

Name	1st Qtr	2nd Qtr	3rd Qtr	4th Qtr	Total
Torres	19	20	33	20	92
Davis	22	10	20	20	72
Chow	10	16	55	16	97
Gregoris	5	15	21	21	62
Ackerman	16	20	42	20	98
TOTAL	**72**	**81**	**171**	**97**	

Though you will not likely need that many, it is believed that an Excel worksheet can actually hold as many as 65,530 hyperlinks.

To Insert a Link

1. Type the text necessary to create the link.

2. Click on the Insert tab.

3. Select the Links button.

4. Type the text to display.

5. Select the Place in This Document button from the Link to pane.

6. Select the desired worksheet from the Cell Reference window.

7. Choose OK.

Figure 24

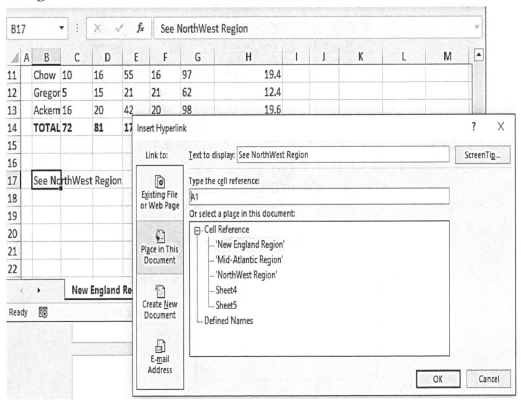

To Edit or Remove a Hyperlink

1. Point to the link and then press your right-mouse button.

2. Select either the Remove Link or Edit Link option from the menu.

Figure 25

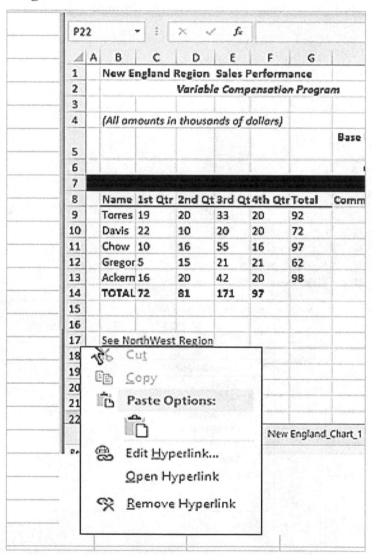

Work Smarter With SmartArt

To create a visually appealing worksheet, consider the use of Microsoft's SmartArt. The SmartArt gallery comes with more than 40 objects including organizational charts, flow charts, and process symbols. SmartArt is a great tool if you need to create infographics. See examples in Figure 26 below.

Inserting SmartArt

1. Select the Insert tab.

2. Place your cursor where you want the object to appear.

3. Click on the SmartArt button.

4. Select a SmartArt graphic, i.e., Process.

5. Choose the desired layout.

6. Click into the placeholders to enter the desired text.

Figure 26

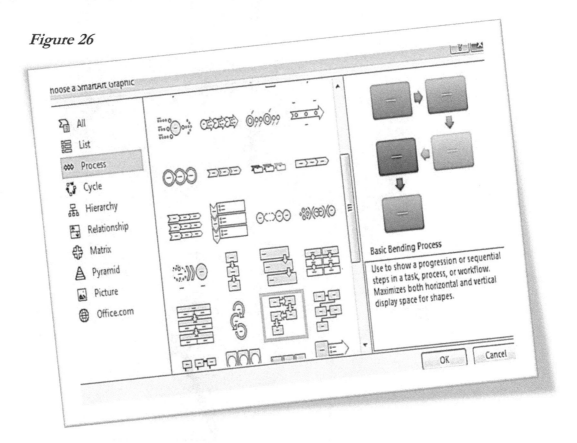

An Example of SmartArt at Work

Using SmartArt to Create Links to Data

Figure 27

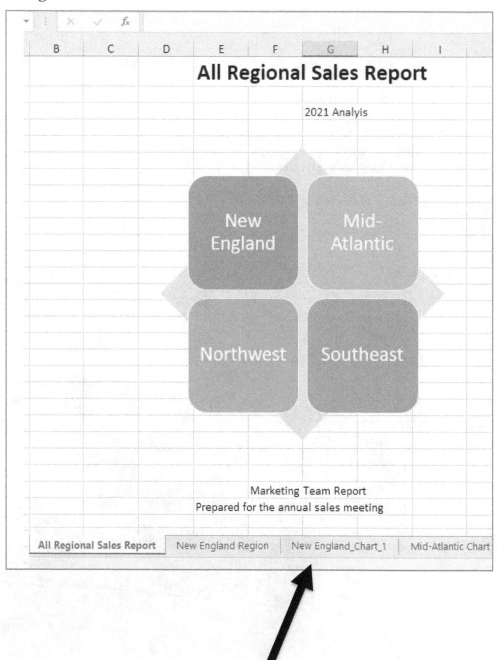

An Application for SmartArt Using Links

SmartArt can be used to not only heighten interest in your worksheet but to focus your reader's attention on a particular set of data. In combination with the Link feature in Excel, you can use SmartArt to direct others to a specific worksheet or existing file located on your computer or network drive. See Figure 27 and notice that I have used SmartArt to create a cover page. The box for each region is a link to a specific worksheet easily created by selecting the box and then choosing the Link command. For a large worksheet with numerous tabs, this kind of linking provides users with another method for finding and opening a worksheet.

Note for example that the Southeast worksheet tab is not immediately visible. The ability to click on the SmartArt link and automatically view that worksheet is a real advantage.

To Insert SmartArt as a Link

1. Select the Insert tab.
2. Choose the SmartArt button.
3. Select the desired graphic.
4. Type the desired text into the SmartArt graphics.
5. Right-click on the graphic to be linked and choose Insert Link.
6. From the Insert Link dialog box, choose Place in this Document.
7. Select the worksheet to be linked.
8. Click on the OK button.

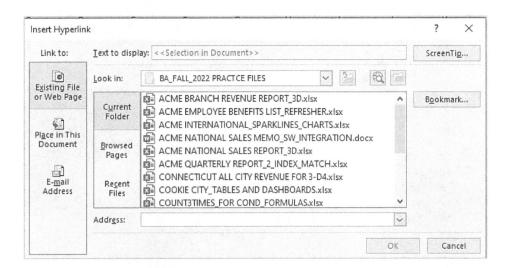

The Insert Hyperlink dialog box.

Working with Shapes

Excel comes with a wonderful assortment of shapes you can use to enhance a worksheet. Whether you need a rectangle, triangle, circle, or star, Excel likely has just what you need. You can find the Shapes button on the Insert tab. See Figure 28 below. Add words to your shape by selecting the shape and then typing the desired text.

To Insert a Shape

1. Click into the cell where you want the shape to appear.

2. Click on the Insert tab.

3. Click on the Shapes drop-down box.

4. Select the desired shape.

5. Hold down your left mouse button and then drag your mouse to draw and size the shape. Optional: Select the shape and then type the desired text.

Figure 28

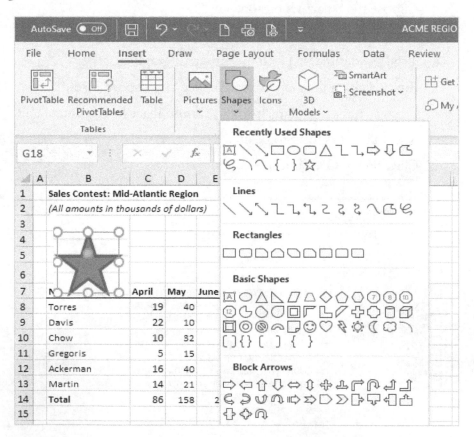

Excel Templates

Microsoft Excel comes bundled with a variety of templates you are sure to appreciate having at your fingertips. For example, if you need an invoice, packing slip, receipt, budget, or income statement, you will likely find them in Excel's templates gallery. Templates are real-time-savers and worth exploring. In addition, you can customize them to fit your needs. For example, if you find an invoice, you can personalize it by adding your company name or logo. You can also change a template's default colors. To search for a template, i.e., flyer, invoice, etc., enter the category into the Search for online templates field.

Viewing and Selecting an Excel Template

1. Click on the File tab.
2. Select the New menu option.
3. Select the desired template.
4. Choose the Create button.

Figure 29

How Templates Can Save You Time

As you will see, Excel templates are easy to work with, can be edited, and can save you from having to create complicated documents from scratch.

You can also personalize a template by simply typing within the pre-designed fields. Thus, it is important to examine your templates, as many of them are designed with formulas that will automatically calculate items such as totals, interest, tax, etc. Some of the templates I have found particularly helpful in Excel include receipts, invoices, and budgets. Take some time to practice working with this great time-saving feature.

Figure 30

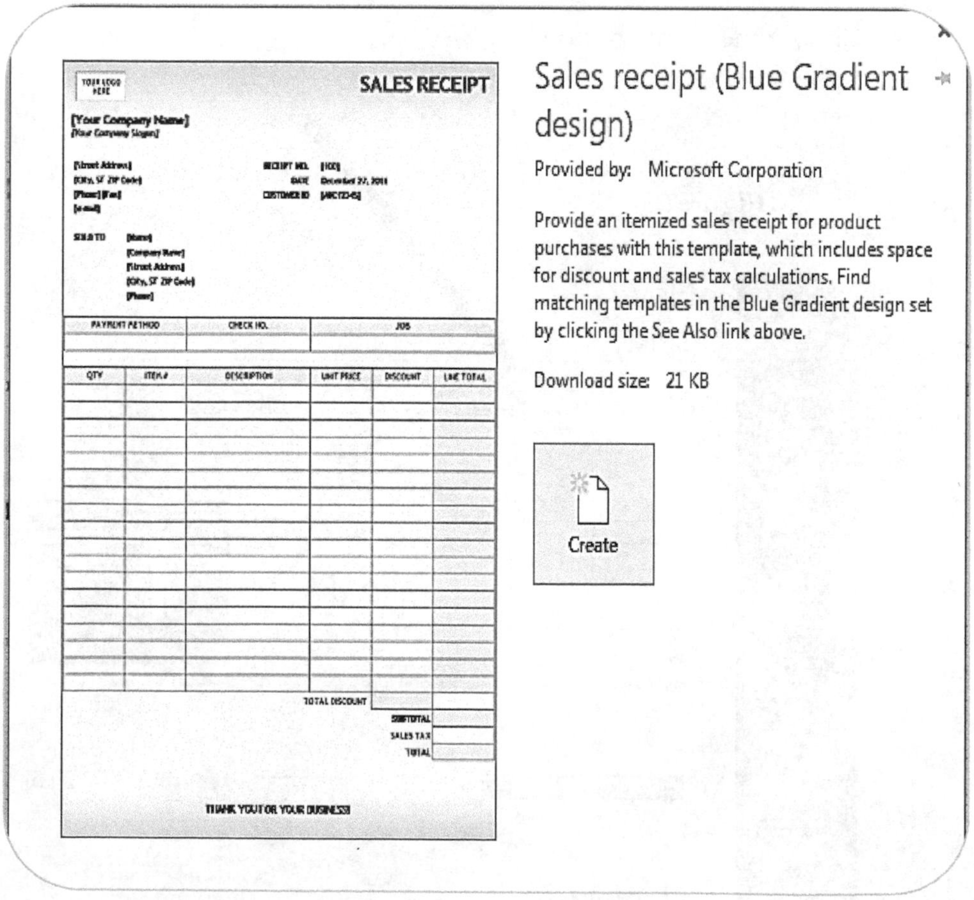

Draw Perfectly With Excel

New with Office 365 is the Draw tab. There you will find free-hand drawing tools that will enable you to mark up your worksheet. Choose from the various pens and highlighter options. You can also control the thickness of the tool by selecting the + or − sign. Notice I have drawn a circle around cell C:14. See Figure 31 below.

To use the free-hand drawing feature, click on the desired drawing tool, and then drag with your mouse to create the figure. It is very similar to creating shapes. To turn off mark-up mode just press your Esc key.

Figure 31

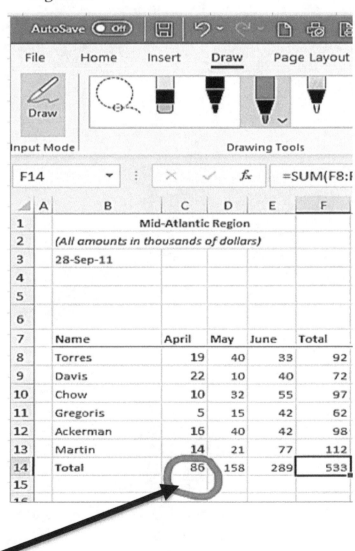

My Notes:

Chapter 5

NAVIGATING BACKSTAGE

- Backstage View

- Info Options

- Excel Properties

- Sharing Worksheet Data

- Exporting Files

- Account Options

- The Options Menu

- Ribbons and Tabs

Introduction to the Backstage Menu

Clicking on the File tab will take you to Excel's Backstage menu. From the Backstage you can examine properties for your workbook, such as file size, tags, and categories. You will also find several menu options such as Info, Open, Save As, and Print. The Info menu option will enable you to control the types of changes others can make to your worksheet when sharing it. In addition, you will find an online Help program if you need more information regarding an Excel feature or function.

On the pages that follow you will become acquainted with the various menu options available within the Backstage window. You might even think of the Backstage window as a dashboard that will enable you to do everything from opening a new file to exporting your worksheet data to another application.

Figure 32

Info Menu Options

Menu Item	Description
Info	⟨ Upload ⟩ ⟨ Share ⟩ ⟨ Copy path ⟩ ⟨ Open file location ⟩ • Select Upload to copy the worksheet to OneDrive. • Choose Share to email the worksheet and/or create a PDF. • Select Copy path to copy the path of your worksheet location, i.e., C:\Reports\Regional Sales. This moves it to the clipboard and lets you paste it into a worksheet or document. • Choose Open file location to open your browsing window to the folder containing your existing file.
Protect Workbook ⌄	Click on the Protect Workbook dropdown box to view options for applying security controls to your file. This is particularly useful when you need to share your workbook with others.
Check for Issues ⌄	Select the Check for Issues dropdown box to view among other things options for inspecting your document. For example, you can use this feature to remove personal information from your worksheet.
Version History	Use the Version History feature if it is important for you to restore and/or track previous versions of your workbook.
Manage Workbook ⌄	Select the Manage Workbook dropdown box to view any recent unsaved files.
Browser View Options	Select Browser View Options if for example you work in a SharePoint environment and need others to view your worksheets through an Internet browser.

Understanding Properties in Microsoft Excel

Properties is a file management feature common to all Microsoft Office applications. Viewing the properties of any given file is easily accomplished by choosing Info from the File tab. Properties as you can see from Figure 33 below displays important information about your file including its size, creation date, and author. Additionally, you can learn not only the date a file was last modified but the identity of the individual who modified it. Furthermore, you can modify file properties by adding a title and a tag that describes the file. By clicking on the Properties dropdown box as depicted in Figure 34, you can view and enter editable fields on the Summary tab.

Figure 33

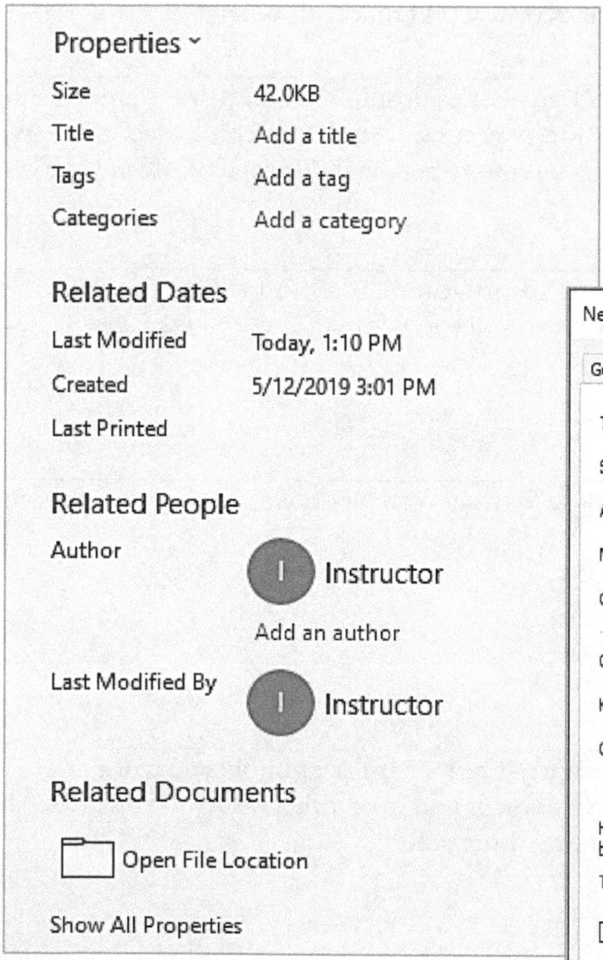

Figure 34

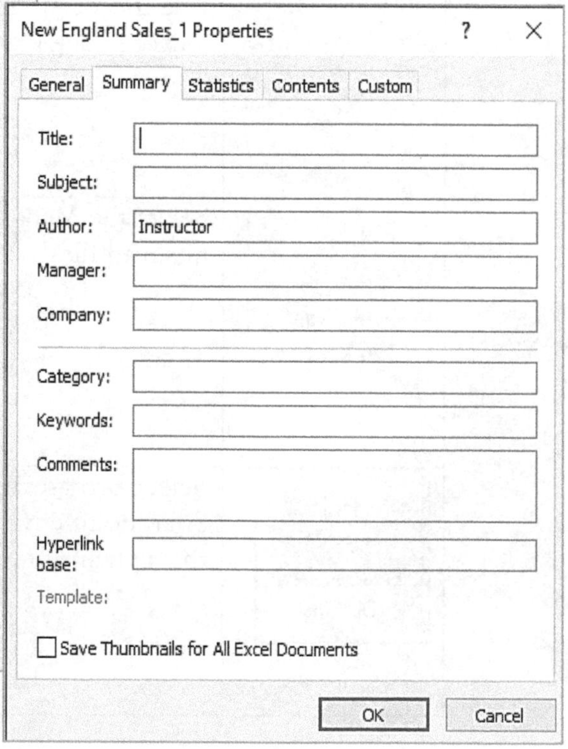

Sharing Worksheet Data

Choosing Share from the Backstage view will cause Excel 365 to display a window like that depicted in Figure 35 below. Notice the Excel prompt to upload a copy of the workbook to OneDrive. This requires that you have an existing OneDrive account. Recall that OneDrive is Microsoft's cloud-based application. If you are using Excel 365 at work, you will want to determine whether the organization wants you to place files on OneDrive. Alternatively, note that through the Share option you can attach a copy of your workbook and email it, or you can create a PDF.

Figure 35

Exporting Worksheet Data

If you work with Excel long enough, you will eventually find yourself wanting to export your worksheet data to other applications. Moreover, you will also no doubt appreciate the ability to control how fonts, images, and formatting appear when opened on a colleague or client's computer. For this reason, you may find the Export feature located on the Backstage menu very useful.

See Figure 36 below and notice the two Export options. The first option will convert your workbook to a PDF file. This is ideal when it is important to ensure that the layout, formatting, fonts, and images in your document not be changed by the recipient. Notice the description states that "Content can't be easily changed." Keep in mind that Microsoft Office 365 can open and make editable PDF files. This feature merely makes it more difficult to do.

Figure 36

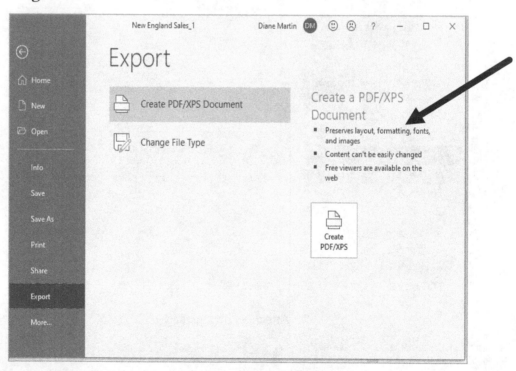

More About Exporting Worksheet Data

Changing File Types

When you select the Change File Type option, Excel displays several file-saving options. This feature is particularly useful if, for example, you need to convert your worksheet to a lower-level version of Excel. This may become necessary because you or a colleague will be working with the file on a computer that is not running the latest version of Excel. Furthermore, some third-party applications will permit you to upload your Excel worksheet data to their systems but require that the file be converted to a CSV (comma delimited) or text format. See Figure 37 below for a list of the available file types.

I recommend that before you experiment with the Change File Type option you save a copy of the worksheet to be converted under a different name. This way you can be sure that you do not alter the original file format.

Figure 37

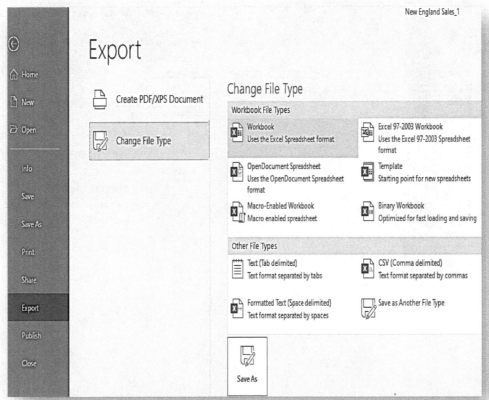

Publishing Your Workbook

The Publish feature within Excel 365 is a powerful tool and subject that goes beyond the scope of this book. However, when you become a more proficient user of Excel you will likely find that Power BI, the business analytics service powered by Microsoft can assist you with manipulating and managing large amounts of data through the use of its interactive visualization features. See Microsoft.com for more information.

Figure 38

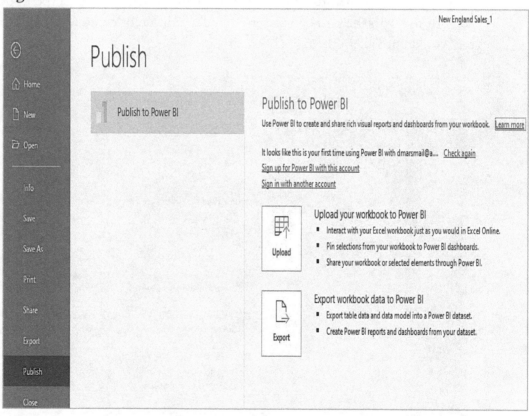

Working with Account Menu Options

Through the Account menu, you can modify privacy settings and control the kinds of content that can be downloaded to your computer. Through the Account menu, you can also control updates to the Excel application and check out any new features that may have been added. Additionally, you can change the background and Office Theme on your computer. You might think of themes as merely a decorative image that appears on the title bar of each application. Note, however, that any change to the theme is made globally. In other words, the selected theme will appear in other Office applications.

The Account menu is just one way to personalize settings in Microsoft Excel. In the next chapter, you will find an explanation of the Options menu. It too is designed to enable you to customize the Excel environment.

Figure 39

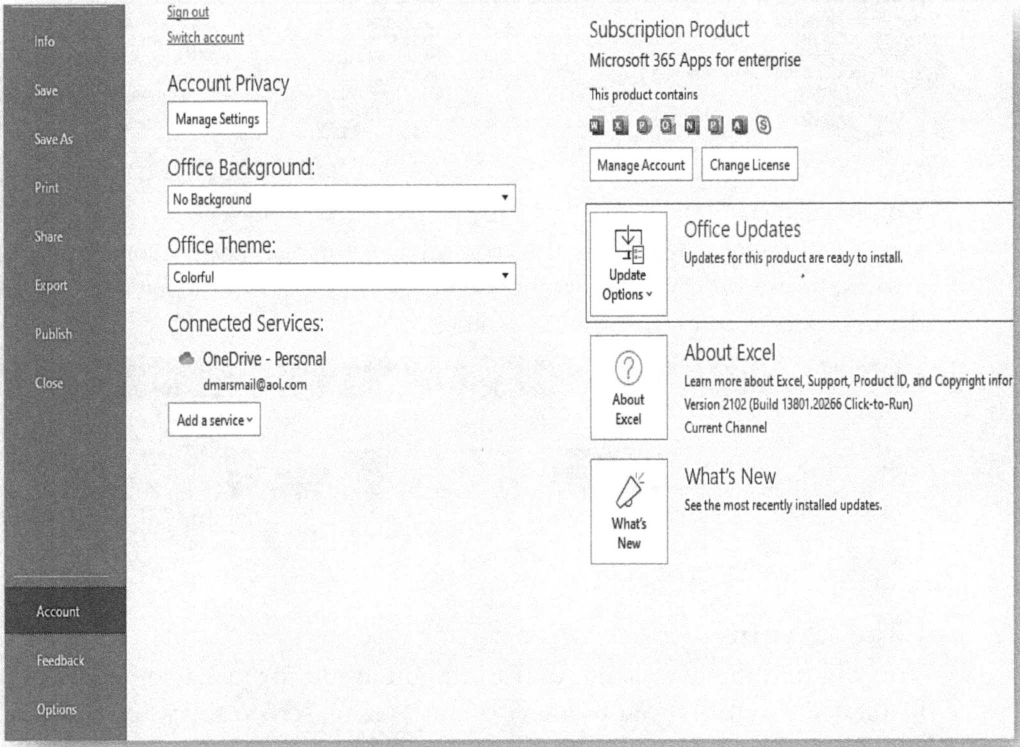

Home

On this ribbon are features you will need frequently. For example, here you can change your font, copy, paste, or apply the number, comma, or currency style to your cells. In addition, don't forget the handy Autosum feature is located here as well. Use AutoSum for instance to quickly add a range of numbers.

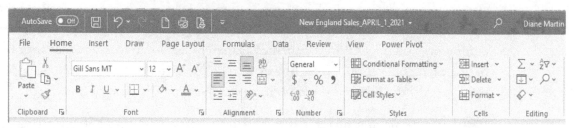

Insert

Use Insert tab functions to place a chart, pictures, headers, and/or footers into your worksheet. Also available are tables, hyperlinks, shapes, and WordArt.

Draw

Use the Drawing tools on this ribbon to enhance and focus attention on specific information within your worksheet data. A wide variety of pens and highlighters make the creation of free-hand objects a cinch.

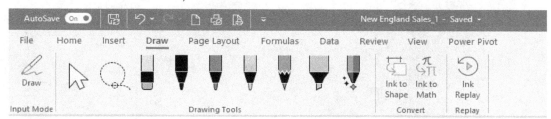

Page Layout

You will find the commands on this ribbon useful for managing how your worksheet is formatted. Control the appearance of gridlines on screen and when printed. Additionally, you can set margins, and page orientation here.

Formulas

Commands on this ribbon can help you quickly calculate worksheet data. AutoSum is just one example of how you apply automated functions like Sum, Average, Min, and Max. See the Function Library for assistance with using more advanced functions like VLOOKUP and IF. If you want to create intuitive labels for your formulas, you will find the Name Manager particularly helpful.

Data

The Data ribbon contains all the functionality you will need to sort and organize the information in your worksheet. Sort options include both the ascending and descending order buttons. To use advanced features like Goal Seek, see the What-If Analysis feature.

Review

Here is where you will find important features like Excel's Spelling and Thesaurus commands. Other useful tools include the ability to add comments to specific worksheet cells and obtain workbook statistics like the number of charts and formulas in your worksheet. Excel's new Smart Lookup feature will enable you to find the definition of a term or phrase.

View

The View ribbon contains functions like Zoom that will permit you to control the magnification of your document on the screen from 10% to 400%. It will also allow you to choose how to arrange multiple windows, turn on/off gridlines, and manipulate the Freeze Panes button.

Get Help Fast

If you forget how to perform a specific task, do not hesitate to click on the Microsoft Excel Help button, which appears in most dialog boxes. Simply look for the little question mark icon or press your F1 key to activate it. See Figure 40 below.

Figure 40

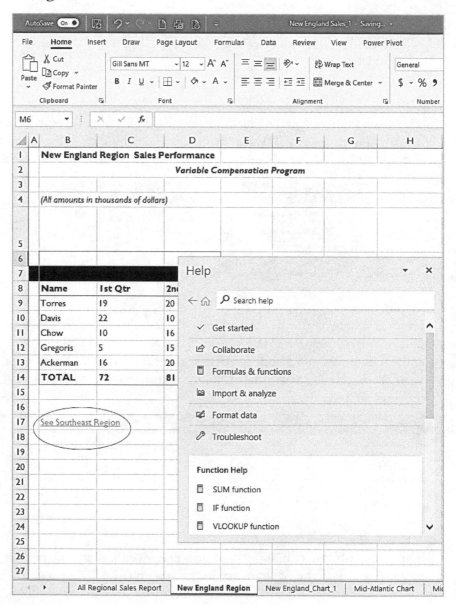

My Notes:

My Notes:

Chapter 6

Navigating the Excel Options Menu

- **Change General Settings**

- **Customize the Ribbon**

- **Change Formula Options**

- **Customize the Quick Access Toolbar**

- **Modify Proofing Options**

- **Customize Save and Backup Settings**

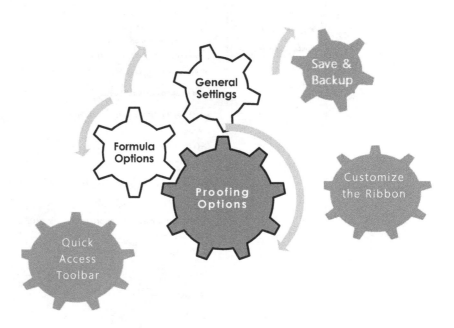

Changing General Settings -- Options Dialog Box

Microsoft Excel comes with certain default settings. For example, when you first began typing in your worksheet, the font was not something you initially chose. A default font was set for you so you could begin typing as soon as you opened the application. However, for a variety of reasons, you may prefer or require a different font. You have the option of changing this and many of the default settings within Excel. To modify these default settings, you will need to access the Options dialog box. See Figure 41.

To begin click on the File tab and choose Options. There are several tabs within this dialog box, and here is where we will begin a brief review of a few of the changes you can make to the Microsoft Excel environment. See the table on the next page for an overview of key general options. Choose the OK button to finalize your selections.

Figure 41

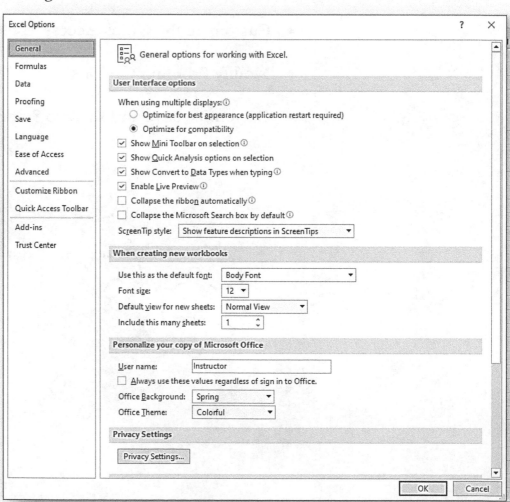

General Options for Working with Excel
Descriptions of Key Options for New Microsoft Excel Users

When using multiple displays	Excel uses this option to ensure maximum contrast and resolution on your screen.
Show <u>M</u>ini Toolbar on selection	When a cell is selected Excel will display the Mini Toolbar to facilitate cell formatting.
Show Quick Analysis options on selection.	When a range of cells is selected, Excel will display various options for manipulating the range, this includes, tables, conditional formatting, charts, and sparklines.
Enable Live Preview	When selected Excel will display a preview of how highlighted data is affected when you hover over different command choices.
Collapse the ribbon automatically	If selected this option will cause Excel to show only ribbon names when you reduce the size of the Excel window.
Collapse the Microsoft Search box by default	This option when selected means that the Search box will not display when Excel is launched. Instead, a magnifying glass representing the Search box will be displayed in the upper right-hand corner of the screen.
Screen Tip Styles	By keeping this option selected Excel will display a little tip about a command when you hover over it with your mouse.

About Other General Options

Creating New Workbooks

As you can see many of the options on the General tab are fairly straightforward. For example, note that the new workbooks segment will enable you to change the default font, and size of your text. Moreover, you can also choose the number of worksheets that are displayed whenever you open Excel.

Personalizing Your Copy of Microsoft Office

Within this segment, you can enter your name which will be preserved in the Properties field for all of your worksheets. If you plan to share your file and need to strip your name from the Properties field, you will want to use the Check for Issues command on the Info menu.

Here within the General tab is another place where you can also change the Office background and Theme as described on Page 53.

Privacy Settings

As is the case on the Account menu, you can modify default privacy settings. Microsoft options related to the collection of diagnostic data downloaded online content, and what they refer to as connected experience data may be modified through the privacy settings button on the General tab.

Start-Up Options

Through these options, you can control the types of Excel files that open on your computer. If you select the Default Programs button, you may be prompted to open Settings>>Apps>>Default Apps on your computer. There is very little need to change the default settings as Excel recognizes older filename extensions unless you are working with another spreadsheet application. Finally, if you do not want to see the Start screen when you launch Excel, deselect this check box.

Figure 42

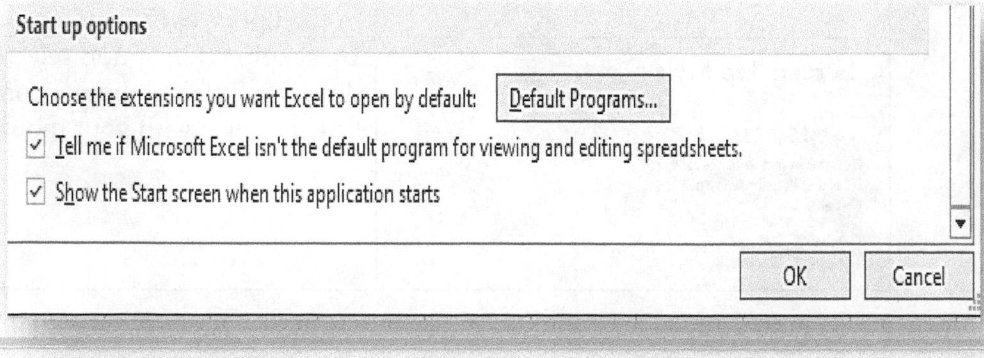

Changing Formula Options

Formula calculation, performance, and error handling may be modified from the Excel Options menu. I recommend you keep the default display and print settings. As you become more proficient in Excel, these options will become more meaningful. For the time being, one basic point of interest includes the default Workbook Calculation option. Note that Automatic is the default setting. This means that whenever a value is changed that affects your formulas Excel will automatically recalculate the workbook. If you prefer that Excel not recalculate because you want to save time until you are finished entering and changing the formulas in your worksheet, then you should select the Manual radio button. See Figure 43 below.

Figure 43

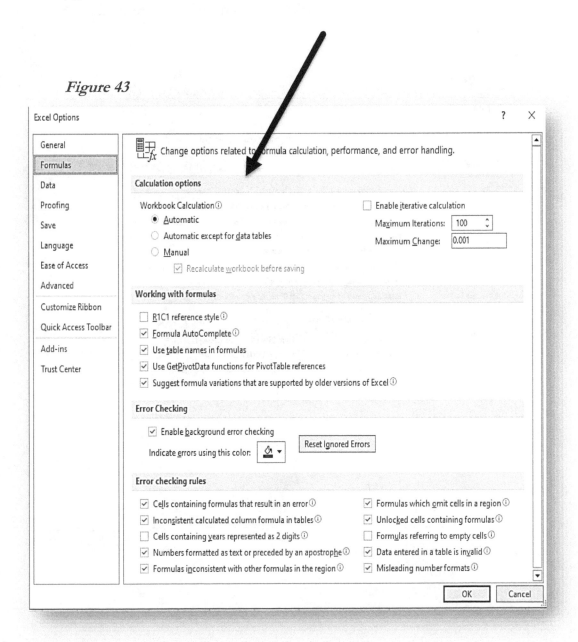

The Significance of Excel Data Options

As this book is intended for readers eager to learn how to perform basic tasks in Microsoft Excel, it is nevertheless useful to have at least a rudimentary understanding of the benefits of what advanced-level features have to offer. As you become a more proficient user of Excel you will no doubt come to appreciate how Excel can help you manage more complex worksheets. Data options within Excel are designed to give the advanced user better control over how large amounts of data can be manipulated in a Pivot table. A Pivot Table is a feature within Excel that can help you with organizing and analyzing data. It is particularly useful when your worksheet contains large amounts of data and you need to create various subgroups of that dataset. An introduction to Pivot Tables is included in Chapter 7. Until you have an actual need to manage large amounts of data, I recommend that you keep the default settings.

Figure 44

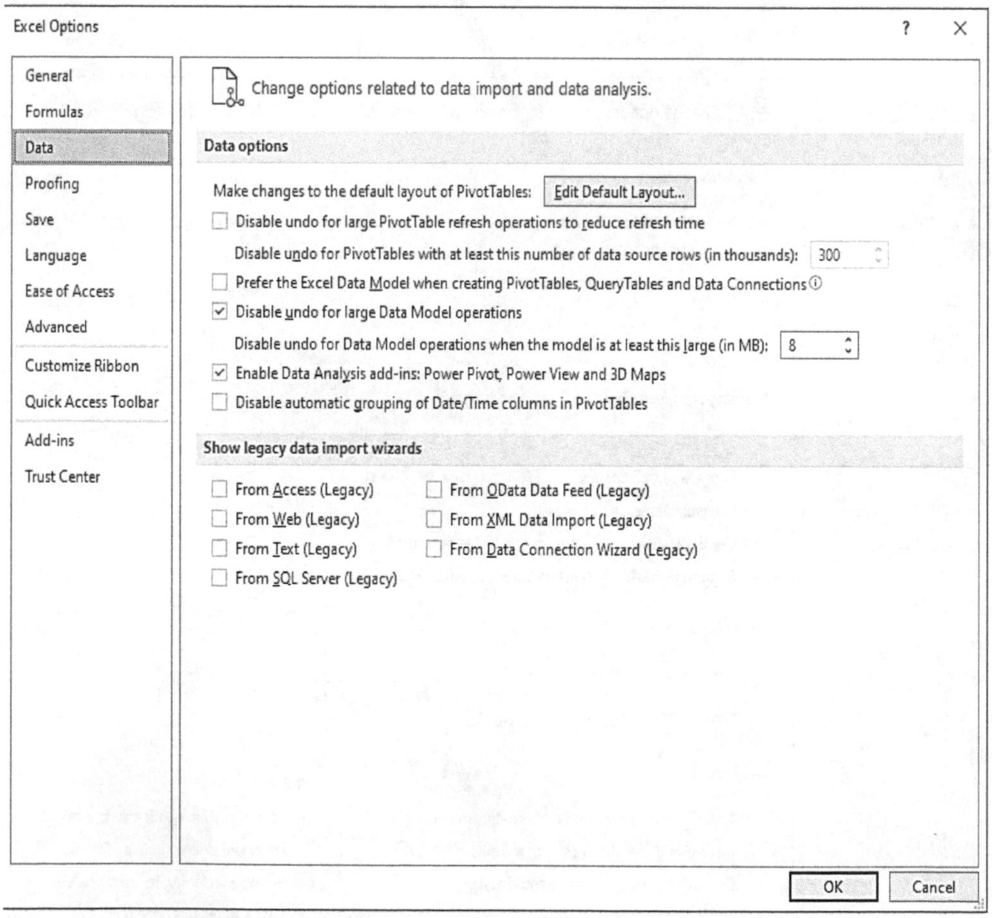

Modify Proofing Options

Behind the Proofing Options, dialog box you can see and change how Excel corrects and formats your text. There are a few basics to consider. Notice that Excel is set by default to ignore words that contain numbers, and to flag repeated words. The default options are indicated by the checkmark (✔). You can turn on or off any of these options by clicking on the checkbox. See Figure 45 below.

In addition, the AutoCorrect database contains frequently misspelled and mistyped words; however, you can add your list of words by typing those words into the "Replace" and "With" fields. Note that if you frequently use terms that might be flagged as misspelled, try creating a custom dictionary. Just click on the Custom Dictionaries button, and you will be prompted to enter words those words that should not be flagged.

Figure 45

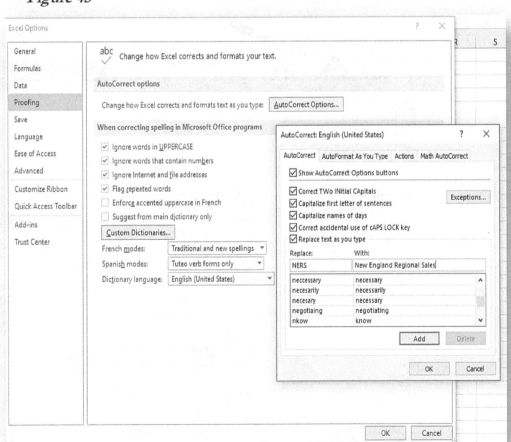

Save Options

As you may know, a worksheet exists in your computer's memory until you save it to some permanent media. Should the power to your computer be interrupted, the worksheet that took you hours to build may be lost forever. Thus, it's a good idea to periodically stop and save your work to your network or hard drive. Fortunately, for subscribers of Office 365, the AutoSave feature will save you from having to remember to save your work. If you subscribe to Office 365 you should see the word AutoSave followed by an On button in the top left-hand corner of your Excel window. See Figure 46 below. With AutoSave enabled Excel automatically saves your workbook to the hard drive or OneDrive every 10 minutes. Thus, it is highly recommended that you keep the AutoSave box checked.

Additionally, Excel includes an AutoRecover feature designed to both save and recover your workspace should your computer experience a power failure. Note that the default is 10 minutes; however, you can increase or decrease the frequency. Finally, you can disable AutoRecover if necessary. Note the checkbox in the figure below. Keep in mind however that if you disable AutoRecover and you do experience a power outage, Excel will not be able to recover your file.

Figure 46

Customizing the Ribbon

You can customize Excel ribbons through this menu option. From the Excel Options menu, you can choose to add or delete commands. For example, if you need the email command, simply click on it as depicted in Figure 47, click on the Add >> button, and then choose OK.

Figure 47

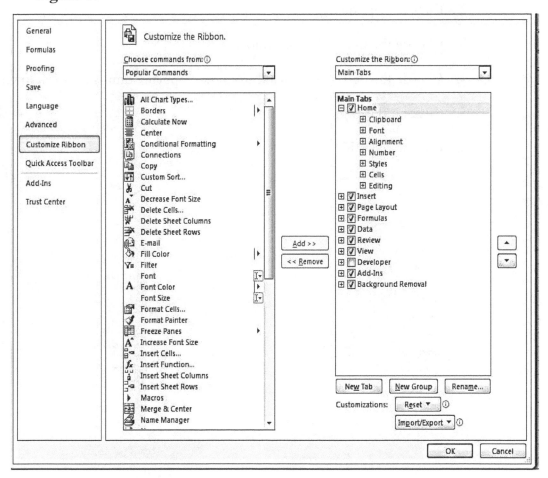

Customizing Your Quick Access Toolbar

Place commands where you can quickly access them by customizing your Quick Access Toolbar. You can find the Quick Access toolbar just below the ribbons on each Microsoft Excel tab. See Figure 48 below.

To Customize the Quick Access Toolbar

1. Select the File Menu.

2. Click on Options.

3. Choose the Quick Access toolbar.

4. Choose the desired command from the Popular Commands dropdown box.

5. Click on the Add>> button.

6. Choose the OK button.

Figure 48

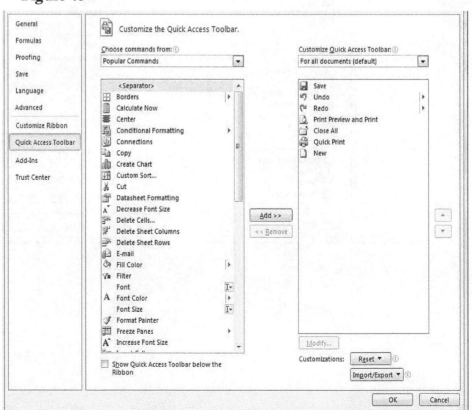

Chapter 7

Introduction to Business Analytics and Advanced Excel Functions

- Create Named Ranges

- Use The Decision-Making IF Function

- Use The VLOOKUP and HLOOKUP Functions

- Create and Edit Charts, Sparklines, and Dashboards

- Insert Sparklines into a Worksheet

- Use the HLOOKUP and MATCH Functions

- Create Pivot Tables and Pivot Charts

- Apply Conditional Formatting

- Add Comments and Notes

- Work with the INDEX and MATCH Functions

- Use the COUNT Functions

- Record Macros and much more.

 Each activity is estimated to take less than six minutes to complete.

Understanding Business Analytics

Increasingly the business community has sought to make better decisions and communicate to their stakeholders the financial condition and prospects of their organizations. For this reason, the subject of business analytics has become increasingly important. Decision-makers are looking to learn from not only how the business has done in the past but are constantly analyzing its key performance indicators to ensure the business achieves its objectives.

Often decision-makers will perform data analysis to determine why a particular problem is happening. This is called diagnostic analytics. Descriptive analytics is about the assessment of historical data to understand the dynamics of what has occurred in the past and how that may be contributing to the organization's present situation. Predictive analytics, on the other hand, enables decision-makers to create and present data that forecast future performance. Lastly, Prescriptive analytics uses forecasting to predict the outcome of different actions based on the supporting data. Moreover, the ability to communicate the data to key stakeholders remains an important objective for most organizations today. Creating spreadsheets is one thing, making them understandable is quite another.

There are any number of tools available on the market that facilitate the analysis of numerical or financial data. However, Microsoft Excel is one of the most popular spreadsheet applications in the world. Anyone looking to enter the world of business would be well-advised to have more than a rudimentary understanding of Microsoft Excel.

The fact is that business analytics is a necessary means of managing data, and a solid understanding of not only what business analytics is as well as a strong foundation in advanced Excel functions will serve you throughout your career. It has been my experience teaching this subject that understanding advanced Excel functions improves one's critical thinking, and that too is a skill that within today's workplace is very much in demand.

This chapter is designed to introduce students with basic knowledge of Microsoft Excel to several advanced functions and formulas they will likely come across at work. I cannot emphasize enough the fact that the only way to develop one's proficiency in advanced Excel is to practice, practice, practice.

Working with Named Ranges

Anyone who has worked with Microsoft Excel knows that cells are referred to by their coordinating row and column address. For example, if we want to add a range of numbers say from F8 to F12 we might indicate that by using the formula =Sum (F8:F12); most of the time this is exactly what we want. However, as your worksheet becomes more complex, you may find it useful to refer to ranges more intuitively. We could for example refer to that same range of cells F8:F12 as "Total." Thus, our formula would look like the following:

=Sum(Total)

Naming a cell or range of numbers is easy to do and can make a worksheet more meaningful for both the person who creates it as well as anyone else that may have to work with that sheet. The first step to creating a named range is to first identify and select the range of cells. Next, you will give the range a meaningful name. Do not include any spaces in the name. See Figure 49 below.

To Create a Named Range

1. Select the range, i.e., "Total".

2. Click into the Name box.

3. Type the name of the range (no spaces) and then press the Enter key.

Figure 49

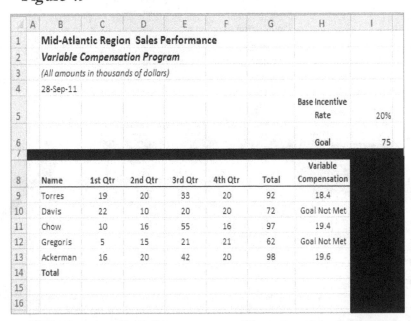

	A	B	C	D	E	F	G	H	I
1		Mid-Atlantic Region Sales Performance							
2		*Variable Compensation Program*							
3		*(All amounts in thousands of dollars)*							
4		28-Sep-11							
5								Base Incentive Rate	20%
6								Goal	75
7									
8		Name	1st Qtr	2nd Qtr	3rd Qtr	4th Qtr	Total	Variable Compensation	
9		Torres	19	20	33	20	92	18.4	
10		Davis	22	10	20	20	72	Goal Not Met	
11		Chow	10	16	55	16	97	19.4	
12		Gregoris	5	15	21	21	62	Goal Not Met	
13		Ackerman	16	20	42	20	98	19.6	
14		Total							
15									
16									

Managing Named Ranges

Named ranges can also be created and managed through Excel's Defined Name group. You will find the Defined Name group located on the Formulas ribbon. To determine whether a worksheet you have inherited contains named ranges, simply click on the Formulas tab, and then the Name Manager button. Alternatively, you can click on the Show formulas button.

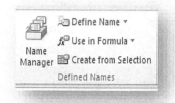

From the Name Manager, you can create, edit, or delete existing ranges. For example, notice in the figure below, that the Name Manager lists three named ranges. To delete a range, you must select the range and then click the delete button.

Keep in mind that deleting a named range may negatively affect the formulas within your worksheet that depend on or refer to that named range. In addition to the functionality described above, you may find the Name Manager useful for documenting the rationale, purpose, or function of a particular range name. If you want to comment about the rate, for example, double-click the named range. Excel will then open a comment window. After you type your comment, others will then be able to read it when they double-click on the range name.

Figure 50

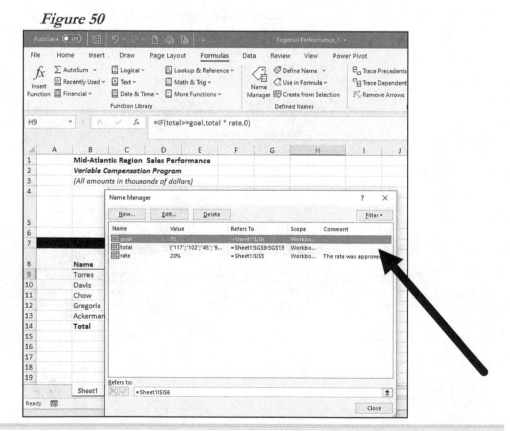

An Example of Named Ranges

If you examine the worksheet below you will see that the content of cell G9 includes a formula consisting of three named ranges, Total, Goal, and Base_Rate. Referring to a range of cells using names instead of cell addresses makes formulas easier to understand. Even a single cell can be named as is the case with cells H5 and H6.

As a beginning Excel user, you may not need to create named ranges, but you will at least want to be familiar with them, as you will eventually come across them in the workplace. In this next lesson, I'll discuss how to combine the use of named ranges with the decision-making IF function.

Figure 51

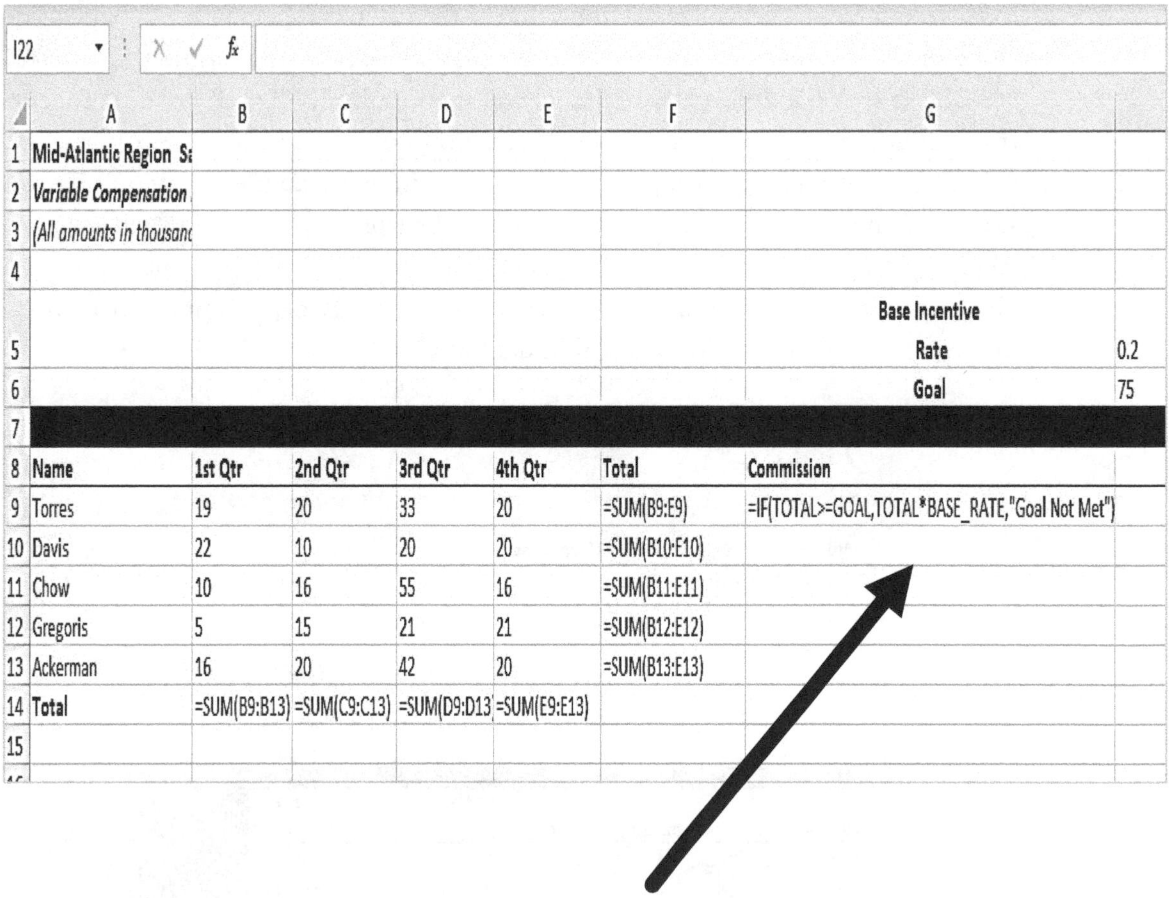

	A	B	C	D	E	F	G	
1	Mid-Atlantic Region Sa							
2	Variable Compensation							
3	(All amounts in thousanc							
4								
5							Base Incentive Rate	0.2
6							Goal	75
7								
8	Name	1st Qtr	2nd Qtr	3rd Qtr	4th Qtr	Total	Commission	
9	Torres	19	20	33	20	=SUM(B9:E9)	=IF(TOTAL>=GOAL,TOTAL*BASE_RATE,"Goal Not Met")	
10	Davis	22	10	20	20	=SUM(B10:E10)		
11	Chow	10	16	55	16	=SUM(B11:E11)		
12	Gregoris	5	15	21	21	=SUM(B12:E12)		
13	Ackerman	16	20	42	20	=SUM(B13:E13)		
14	Total	=SUM(B9:B13)	=SUM(C9:C13)	=SUM(D9:D13)	=SUM(E9:E13)			
15								

The Decision-Making IF Function

Microsoft Excel makes it possible to construct a formula that will place within a cell a certain value when a condition is true. Alternatively, if the condition that Excel checks for is false, another value will be returned. Essentially Excel is performing what is referred to as a logical test.

One popular application of the IF function is to use it to check whether some numerical goal has been met. For example, suppose you want to pay a commission to a salesperson who made his or her quarterly sales quota. Naturally, if the salesperson does not make their goal, you will not likely want to pay them anything. You could use Excel to calculate and display the commission that all salespeople who made the quota should receive. See Figure 52 below.

Consider the following formula: **=IF(Total>=Goal, Total*Base_Rate,0)**

In this example, Excel will check the value of the cell or range named "Total" to determine whether the content of that cell is greater than or equal to the content of the cell named "Goal." If that condition is true, Excel will then multiply "Total" by the "Incentive Rate. If the condition is false, Excel will place a zero in our result cell. The commas are used to delimit each task Excel must perform. Note that in our example below only Torres, Chow, and Ackerman have earned a commission because they met or exceeded the goal. Alternatively, Excel displays the words "Goal Not Met" in the result cell for Davis and Gregoris; this is exactly the result we want. Note that Excel will print into a resulting cell the text or number that appears within quotation marks.

Figure 52

	A	B	C	D	E	F	G	H	I
1		Mid-Atlantic Region Sales Performance							
2		*Variable Compensation Program*							
3		*(All amounts in thousands of dollars)*							
4		28-Sep-11							
5								Base Incentive Rate	20%
6								Goal	75
7									
8		Name	1st Qtr	2nd Qtr	3rd Qtr	4th Qtr	Total	Variable Compensation	
9		Torres	19	20	33	20	92	18.4	
10		Davis	22	10	20	20	72	Goal Not Met	
11		Chow	10	16	55	16	97	19.4	
12		Gregoris	5	15	21	21	62	Goal Not Met	
13		Ackerman	16	20	42	20	98	19.6	
14		Total							
15									
16									

Construction of an IF Statement

If you find the IF function is a little confusing, do not worry. I recommend that you initially start by writing out exactly what you want the application to do. After you have done this a few times, you will find the process relatively straightforward, and you will be able to do it in your head. Let us consider another example. Suppose a teacher has set up her grade book in Excel. Final student grades must be represented by a letter. The teacher has decided to give a final grade of A to any student who has achieved an overall average of 85 or higher on the final exam, and a B to all the others. How might she use the IF function to help her track and report these grades? Let's practice writing out our formula.

Our very simple logical test would look like the following:

=IF(C2>=$F$1,"A", "B")

This formula simply instructs Excel to check if the value in C2 is greater than or equal to the value in F1 (85). That is the first condition. If that condition is met, Excel must print "A" in the result cell. If the condition is not met, Excel must print a "B". Note the use of an absolute reference in cell F1.

Figure 53

	A	B	C	D	E	F	G
						=IF(C2>=$F$1,"A", "B")	
1	Student		Final Exam Grade	Final Grade	Letter Grade	85	A
2	Michele		95	A	Letter Grade	80	B
3	Sammy		85				
4	Thomas		79				
5	Robert		89				
6	Jeanie		98				
7	Wille		78				
8	Terri		75				
9	Joan		80				
10	Jack		88				
11	Annette		77				
12							

The Finished Gradebook

Figure 54

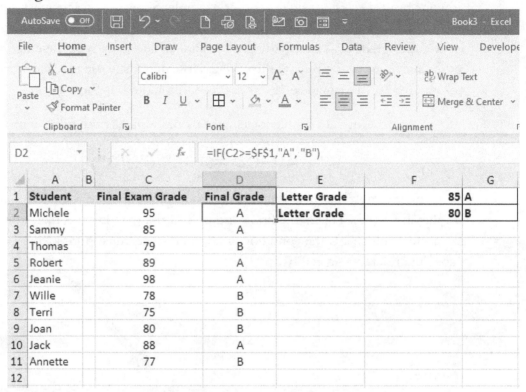

While this example is fairly easy, the use of the IF function can become quite complex. You may find the Insert Function feature particularly useful when you need help constructing a more complex formula. The Insert Function feature will step you through the formula. You will become more familiar with Insert Function during the next lesson on using VLOOKUP.

Creating a Simple Logical Test

Below are the steps for using the Insert Function feature when you are constructing a formula with a decision-making IF statement. See Figure 55.

To Create a Logical Test

1. Place your cursor in the result cell.

2. Select the Formulas tab.

3. Choose Logical from the Function Library Group.

4. Click on the IF menu option.

5. Type the logical test.

6. Type the calculation or text you want to be displayed in the Value_if_true field.

7. Type the calculation or text you want to be displayed in the Value if_false field.

8. Click OK.

9. Use the Fill handle to copy down.

Figure 55

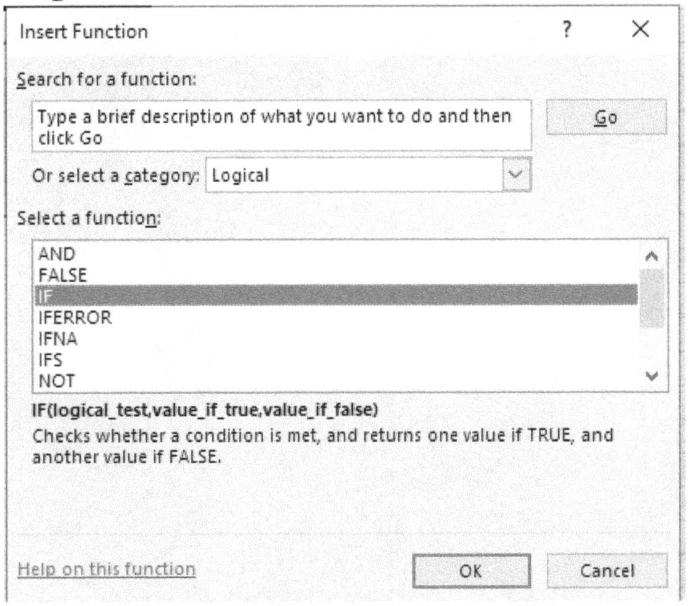

My Notes:

Introduction to the V-LOOKUP Function

The Vertical Lookup or VLOOKUP function as it is commonly referred to may be used whenever you want Excel to look up and report a specific value found within a vertically aligned table. Recall that we previously used the IF function for a class of students who would earn either one of two grades. In this scenario, assume that as a teacher I want a grade book that will accurately represent each student's grades. To determine the final letter grade, I need Excel to examine a table containing letter grades, match them against the student's exam average, and return the appropriate letter grade. Examine my grade book in Figure 56.

Figure 56

	A	B	C	D	E	F	G	H	I
	Grade book								
1	A	B	C	D	E	F	G	H	I
	Student Name	Exam 1	Exam 2	Exam 3	Exam 4	Student Average	Final Letter Grade	Grade Look-up Table	
2	Michele	95	85	88	92	90		0	F
3	Sammy	85	75	78	77	78.75		60	D
4	Thomas	79	76	73	72	75		70	C
5	Robert	89	90	92	95	91.5		80	B
6	Jeanie	98	97	85	80	90		90	A
7	Willie	78	65	60	63	66.5			
8	Terri	75	80	85	86	81.5			
9	Sharon	80	78	62	65	71.25			
10	Boris	82	92	55	50	69.75			
11	Miquel	77	55	65	69	66.5			

Again, here is where named ranges can be particularly useful. To perform this task, I created two named ranges. First, I selected the range F2:F11, and then typed the words **Student_Avg** into the Name Box. Obviously, this range includes the exam averages for each student. Next, I selected the range H2:I6 and then clicked into the Name Box and typed **Grade_Table**.

As you can see, the second named range was created by selecting the cells that make up my **Grade_Table.** It consists of the letter grades and their numerical equivalents. This is what Excel considers a "table array." To work properly, Excel requires that the table be arranged in ascending order.

Now I am ready to use the VLOOKUP function. This function is one of the Look-up and reference functions within Excel. You will find it located on the Formulas tab within the Function Library Group.

To get Excel to look up a value it will be important to ensure that the cursor is placed in the first result cell. In this case that would be cell G2. Next, select the Formulas tab, and then choose the Insert function command. By the way, if you don't see VLOOKUP in the Insert Function window, simply begin typing it in the Search field. After selecting VLOOKUP, the Function Arguments dialog box will open. See Figure 57 below Note that as I enter the named ranges in the Lookup value and Table_array fields, Excel begins calculating the results.

Again, examine the VLOOKUP Function Arguments dialog box below in Figure 57. Notice the column index number field. Here is where Excel is being instructed to look at the <u>second</u> column of the Grade_Table and then display the value found in the same row.

Lastly, choose the OK button to calculate the results.

Figure 57

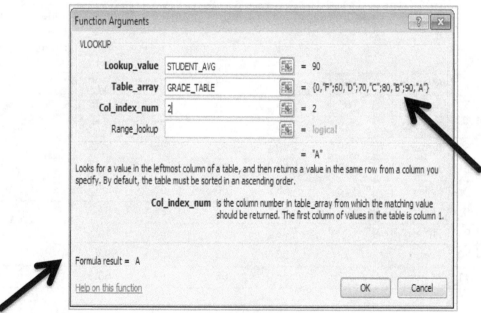

Working successfully with VLOOKUP takes a little practice. Fortunately, Excel can guide you through the process through its Insert Function button. As you can see, when you click on this button and select VLOOKUP, the application will guide you through the formula construction process. You will find the Insert function button located within the Formulas tab.

If you choose to use the Insert function button and are still having difficulty, try clicking on the Help on this function link located within the Function Arguments dialog box.

The Finished Grade Book

As you can see from Figure 58, the grade book more accurately reflects student grades based on their exam average. As a point of reference, keep in mind that the grade table can be expanded to include other grading variations such as A-/A+, B- /B+, etc.

Figure 58

	A	B	C	D	E	F	G	H	I
			Grade book						
1	A	B	C	D	E	F	G	H	I
	Student Name	Exam 1	Exam 2	Exam 3	Exam 4	Student Average	Final Letter Grade	Grade Look-up Table	
2	Michele	95	85	88	92	90	A	0	F
3	Sammy	85	75	78	77	78.75	C	60	D
4	Thomas	79	76	73	72	75	C	70	C
5	Robert	89	90	92	95	91.5	A	80	B
6	Jeanie	98	97	85	80	90	A	90	A
7	Willie	78	65	60	63	66.5	D		
8	Terri	75	80	85	86	81.5	B		
9	Sharon	80	78	62	65	71.25	C		
10	Boris	82	92	55	50	69.75	D		
11	Miquel	77	55	65	69	66.5	D		

The VLOOKUP function can be a valuable time-saver.

The HLOOKUP Function

HLOOKUP is one of several Microsoft Excel lookup and reference functions. While VLOOKUP is great for vertically aligned data, HLOOKUP comes in handy when your values are horizontally aligned, and you need it to return a value by looking across a specified number of rows. In the example below, I have a worksheet set up to enable me to quickly track and report what I have in inventory on any given day. The formula in B12 gets Excel to look across a row of data and return the exact value.

My formula =**HLOOKUP("MARKERS", B1:H8,2,0)** instructs Excel to search the range B1:H8, then look across the second row and retrieve the value in that cell.

Figure 59

	A	B	C	D	E	F	G	H
				fx	=HLOOKUP("MARKERS", B1:H8, 2,0)			
1	DATE	PENCILS	CALENDARS	PAPER	PENS	MARKERS	TAPES	STAPLERS
2	Sept 1st	35	38	37	42	42	25	32
3	Sept 2nd	17	20	25	36	41	20	31
4	Sept 3rd	20	17	14	20	24	22	21
5	Sept 4th	12	28	30	40	36	30	27
6	Sept 5th	29	32	33	33	21	21	18
7	Sept 6th	23	17	19	22	27	27	33
8	Sept 7th	17	20	25	35	22	33	21
9	Total Week 1							
10								
11		Day 1	Day 2	Day 3	Day 4	Day 5	Day 6	Day 7
12	MARKERS Sold	42						
13	PAPER Sold		37					
14	CALENDARS Sold							

You can develop your proficiency in using HLOOKUP. See the Practice Exercises section at the end of the book.

Introduction to the INDEX Function

INDEX is another one of Excel's lookup and reference functions. The INDEX function is great for more complex worksheets when you need greater specificity than what VLOOKUP offers. In this segment, I'll describe how the INDEX function is used to return the value at a given location within a range. For example, let us suppose I need a dynamic formula that will look up the number of pumpkin pies that have been sold. My result cell is E2; there I have entered the following formula.

=INDEX(A2:C10, 2,3)

When Excel sees this formula, it will look at the range, A2:C10 find the intersection of Row 2 and Column 3, and then copy that value to my result cell, E2. Note that the headings in this example do not include the headings, i.e., Pies, Price, Number.

Figure 60

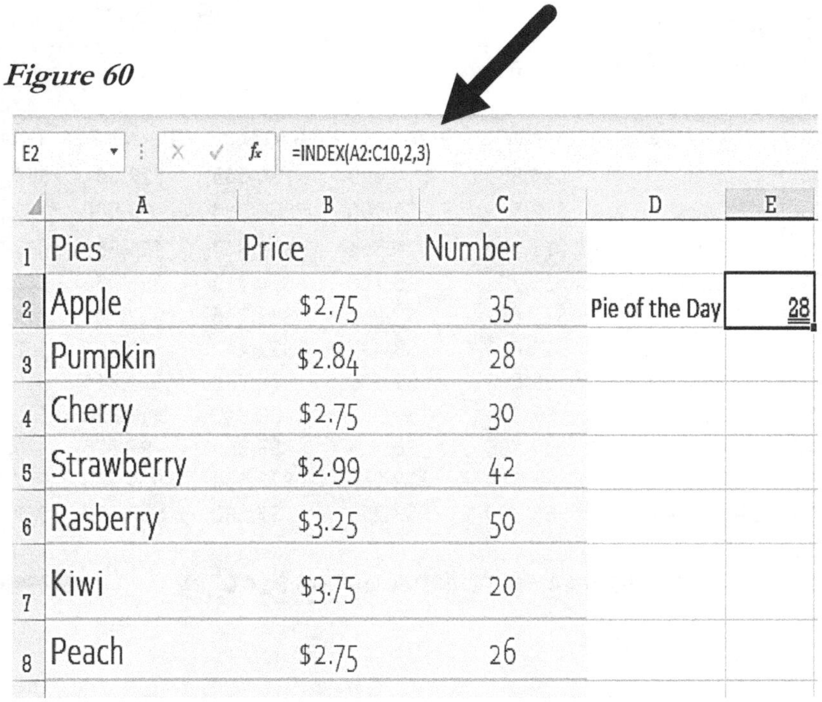

Very often, the INDEX function is used along with the MATCH function. See the next page to learn more about how to combine both functions for greater accuracy.

Develop your proficiency in using the INDEX function. See the Practice Section at the end of the book.

Working with INDEX and MATCH

Nesting functions like INDEX and MATCH can be useful when you need Excel to search a range and retrieve an exact match. It is the job of the MATCH function to find the location of an item within a range. For example, in Figure 61 below you will see a worksheet designed to track three of the Acme sales team's top performers.

Examine the formula in the result cell I4 and notice that this will cause Excel to search the range C4:F14 and then look for a match (the row position)for "Dewey" in the range B4:B14. It then retrieves the corresponding value from Column 2 which represents her Quarter 2 results.

Figure 61

	A	B	C	D	E	F	G	H	I
1		Acme Systems Sales Report							
2									
3		Last Name	Quarter 1	Quarter 2	Quarter 3	Quarter 4	Total	Rep	Dewey
4	1	Abel	$15,885	$14,625	$6,565	$22,354	$59,429	Qtr_2	$ 16,554
5	2	Caine	$12,500	$5,200	$6,384	$5,500	$29,584		
6	3	Dewey	$11,296	$16,554	$13,867	$25,650	$67,367		
7	4	Casar	$5,752	$6,786	$14,752	$15,850	$43,140	Rep	Miranda
8	5	Gaines	$12,699	$7,350	$11,796	$12,600	$44,445	Qtr_3	
9	6	Miranda	$11,652	$8,487	$12,442	$30,525	$63,106		
10	7	Morris	$9,396	$9,589	$8,750	$12,365	$40,100		
11	8	Lane	$7,259	$3,900	$8,845	$10,326	$30,330	Rep	Abel
12	9	Clark	$7,536	$6,183	$3,952	$7,526	$25,197	Qtr_1	
13	10	Olson	11,350	$12,220	$13,500	$15,500	$52,570		
14	11	Cunningham	$8,300	$9,250	$7,580	$12,650	$37,780		
15									
16		=INDEX(C4:F14,MATCH("Dewey",B4:B14,0),2)			←				

Develop your proficiency in using the INDEX and MATCH functions. See the Practice Section in Appendix A.

 There is a whole lot more to learn about the INDEX and MATCH functions. See Online Resources in Appendix C.

Creating Charts with Microsoft Excel

To make numeric data more meaningful to others, consider the use of a chart. Within seconds, you can use Microsoft Excel to insert any one of a variety of chart types into your worksheet. Chart types include line, bar pie, and area to name a few. There are more than 11 available chart types from which to choose. After we complete the worksheet, the next step will be to select the cells to be represented in our chart. Generally, you will not want to include totals among your highlighted cells since that could skew the results. Lastly, we will let Excel recommend the best chart based on the range of cells we have selected. See the Recommended Charts command in Figure 62 below. See the practice exercise for this lesson in the Appendix.

To Create a Chart:

1. Select the cells to be included in your chart. (Do not select totals.)

2. Click on the Insert tab.

3. Click on Recommended Charts located in the Chart group.

4. Select the Clustered Column Chart.

5. Click on the OK button.

Figure 62

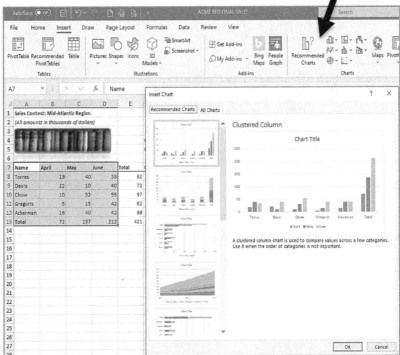

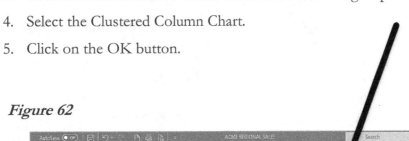

An Example of an Embedded Clustered Column Chart

A real advantage of an embedded chart lies in the ability to move it seamlessly around your worksheet. In addition, through the Chart Design tab, you can quickly apply a new style to your chart.

As you will see, creating a basic embedded chart is fairly easy to do. However, note that Excel comes bundled with several features that can be used to make a chart from a simple to a sophisticated tool for communicating numerical data.

Figure 63

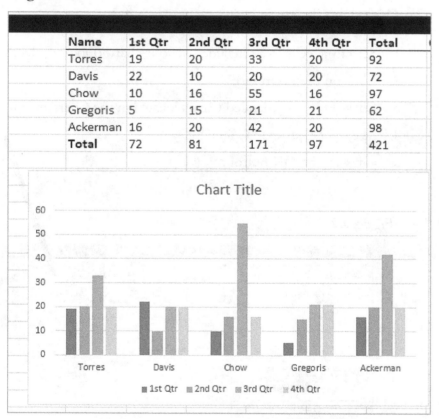

Name	1st Qtr	2nd Qtr	3rd Qtr	4th Qtr	Total
Torres	19	20	33	20	92
Davis	22	10	20	20	72
Chow	10	16	55	16	97
Gregoris	5	15	21	21	62
Ackerman	16	20	42	20	98
Total	72	81	171	97	421

A Simple Embedded Clustered Column Chart

Creating Chart Sheets

One alternative to an embedded chart is the chart sheet. The chart sheet resides on a separate worksheet. See Figure 71 on Page 94. An easy method of creating your chart sheet involves the use of the Move Chart command.

 The first step requires that you click on the border of your chart and then choose the Move Chart menu option. When the Move Chart dialog box opens, select the New sheet button.

Alternatively, if you select the Object in radio button Excel will keep and move your embedded chart intact to another worksheet of your choosing. See Figure 64 below. When you click on the dropdown box, Excel will display other sheets within your workbook. You simply select the desired worksheet and then choose the OK button.

Figure 64

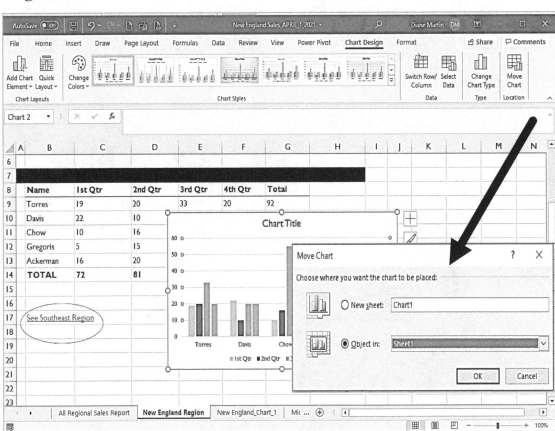

You can move your embedded chart to its own worksheet using the Move Chart command.

Editing a Chart Title

In addition to the ability to move your chart, you can choose to modify such elements as titles, legends, gridlines, axis styles, and colors. Remember, editing your chart requires that you first activate it and you activate a chart by clicking on it. Notice the handles surrounding the chart in Figure 65. These handles indicate that the chart has been activated. Now we can proceed to edit our chart title.

1. Click into the Chart Title placeholder.
2. Type A new title for your chart.

Note the three icons that appear when your chart appears. These commands will enable you to among other things quickly edit your chart's data labels, axis titles, and legends. Additionally, Chart Styles will enable you to quickly change the style and color scheme of your chart. Finally, you can control the data points and names that appear on your chart. For example, the Chart Filter feature allows you to restrict the display of the chart below to just the first and fourth quarter and/or limit the chart display to just two or the five representatives.

Figure 65

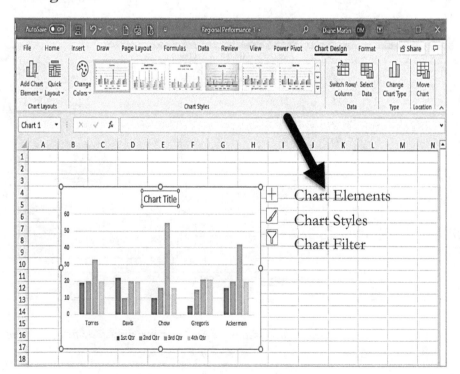

Managing and Editing Excel Charts

When you double-click on your chart, Excel will activate its Chart Design tab. At this point, you can select an alternate chart type as well as edit other chart elements. For example, you can edit the chart title as well as move and/or edit the legend.

Editing the Chart Legend

To move your chart's legend, click on it, and then drag it to the desired location. Alternatively, you can right-click your mouse button and select Format Legend from the short menu. Choose the new position for your legend from the Format Legend dialog box. Note the other options such as Fill, used to modify the color of your legend as well as the Effects button used to add a shadow or glow. See Figure 66.

Figure 66

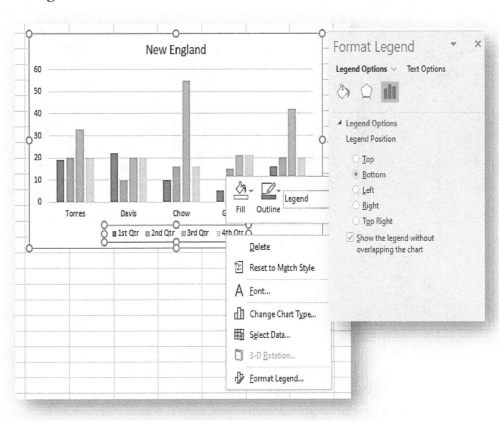

Formatting Chart Labels

You can decide how to display and/or format the horizontal and vertical axis for your chart using the Axis Titles feature.

1. Activate the chart.
2. Click on the Chart Elements button.
3. Select Vertical or Horizontal Axis.

If you select More Legend Options, Excel will open a Format Legend dialog box. There you can choose to modify the colors, fill, and style of your legend.

Applying Gridlines

Gridlines enhance the ability to compare data markers to axis values, by extending the tick marks for an axis across the chart's plot area. See Figure 67. Excel 365 makes it possible to apply these gridlines.

Figure 67

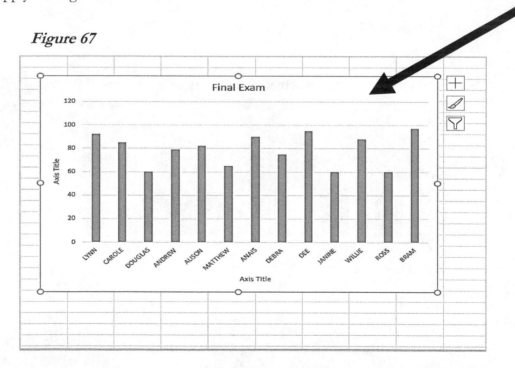

To Add Gridlines

1. Activate the chart.
2. Click on the Chart Elements button.
3. Click on the gridlines button.

To Delete Gridlines

1. Activate the chart.
2. Click on the Chart Elements button.
3. Deselect Gridlines.

Editing Data Labels

Data Labels may be added to a chart to depict individual data points. Data Labels may be represented as values i.e., percentages. For example, look at the pie chart in Figure 68 below, and notice that each data point reflects the salesperson's performance as a percentage of the whole. Furthermore, a chart can be limited to a specific range within your worksheet. For instance, notice that Figure 68 depicts only April sales. See the following steps for editing Data Labels:

1. Activate the chart.
2. Right-click within the chart.
3. Click on the Format Data Labels menu option.
4. Select the desired Label Options.

Figure 68

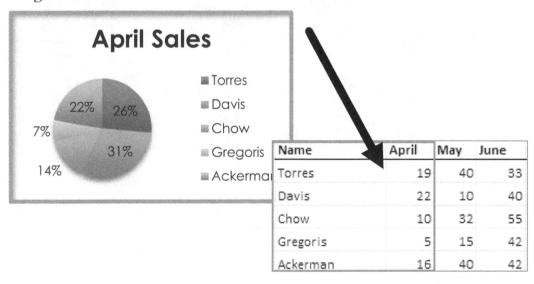

Formatting Data Labels

From the Format Data Labels dialog box, you can select or deselect various elements within your chart. However, you can also edit the fill colors, size, and properties of your data labels. Furthermore, Text Options include the ability to control how data labels appear, i.e., horizontal or vertical. Try experimenting with these options and remember if you make a change and don't like the effect you can always use the Undo command.

Figure 69

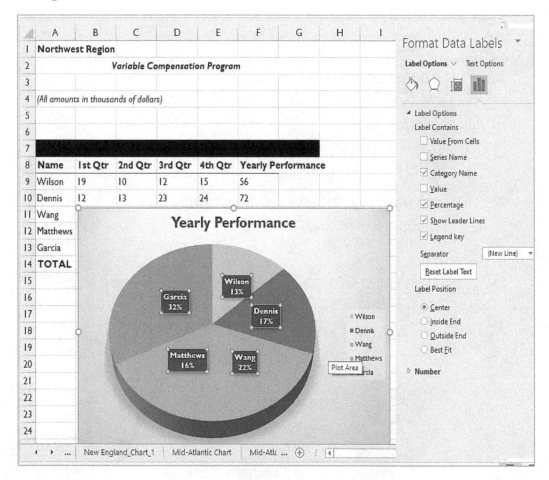

Updating a Chart

As is often the case, you will likely need to update a chart as conditions change. Alternatively, a chart may require updating if something or someone's performance changes. Fortunately, updating a chart is fairly straightforward. The secret lies in the Insert row and Insert column feature. See Figure 70. As you can see, six individuals are listed. Assume that you have transferred to this department from another region. See how easily the chart be updated to include your numbers.

To Update A Chart

1. Insert a row or column for your name.
2. Type the new data, i.e., April = 12, May=24, and June = 33.

Figure 70

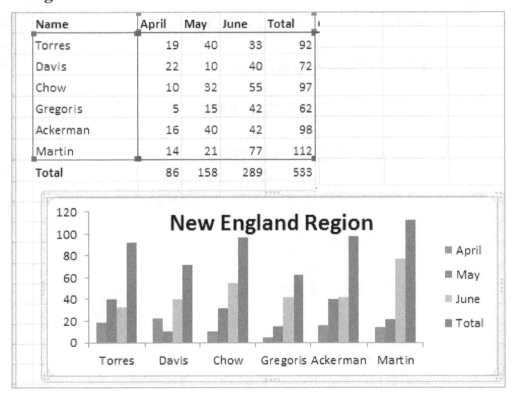

Name	April	May	June	Total
Torres	19	40	33	92
Davis	22	10	40	72
Chow	10	32	55	97
Gregoris	5	15	42	62
Ackerman	16	40	42	98
Martin	14	21	77	112
Total	86	158	289	533

Figure 71

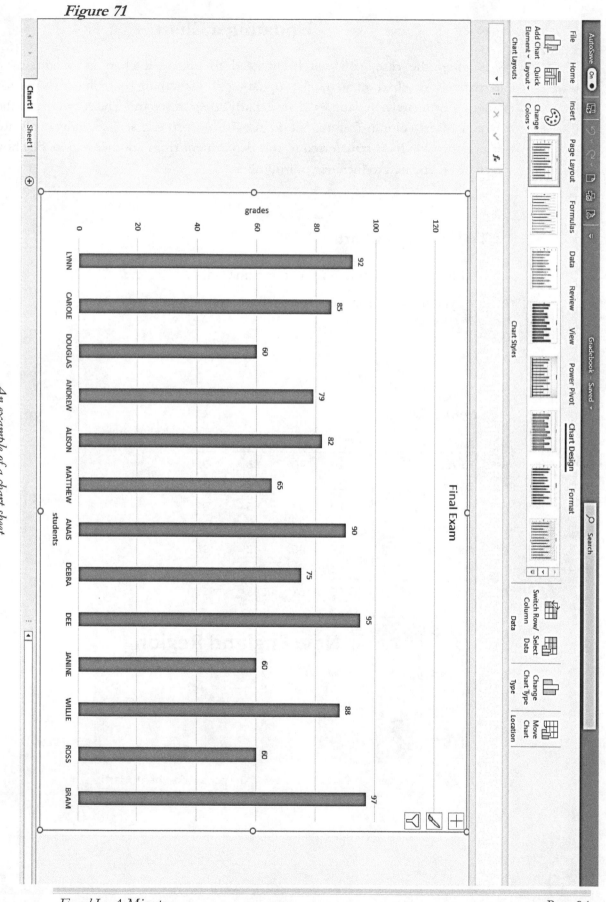

An example of a chart sheet.

Working with Sparklines

The act of converting numerical data into a chart can assist others with interpreting the values. Sparklines is a feature within Excel that will enable you to create a miniature chart within the contents of a single cell. There are three types of Sparklines: Bar, Line, and Win/Loss. You will find that Sparklines can be very useful for showing trends in a series of values. For example, see Figure 72 below and notice the cells adjacent to the Total column are depicting a bar chart for each sales representative's quarterly sales.

When selecting the range for your Sparklines, you will want to avoid picking up the total column as this would skew the results.

To Insert Sparklines

1. Place your cursor where you want to place your Sparklines.

2. Click on the Insert tab.

3. Select the desired Sparklines type, i.e., Line, Column, Win/Loss.

4. Select the range for the Sparklines, i.e., see Figure 68 below).

5. Choose the OK button.

6. Use the Fill handle to complete the range.

Figure 72

Name	QTR 1	QTR 2	QTR 3	Total	Chart
Torres	19	40	33	92	
Davis	22	10	40	72	
Chow	10	32	55	97	
Gregoris	5	15	42	62	
Ackerman	16	40	42	98	
Total	72	137	212	421	

Editing and Deleting Sparklines

As previously mentioned, there are three types of Sparklines. You can easily change them by selecting from the Type group on the Sparklines ribbon. Additionally, you can enhance your Sparklines by selecting from the Style group. As you can see from Figure 73 other options include the ability to change the Sparkline color as well as indicate the high, low, first, and last points when the Line type is selected.

Should you wish to delete the Sparklines in your worksheet, simply select the range, right-click your mouse button, and select the Clear Selected Sparklines menu option.

Figure 73

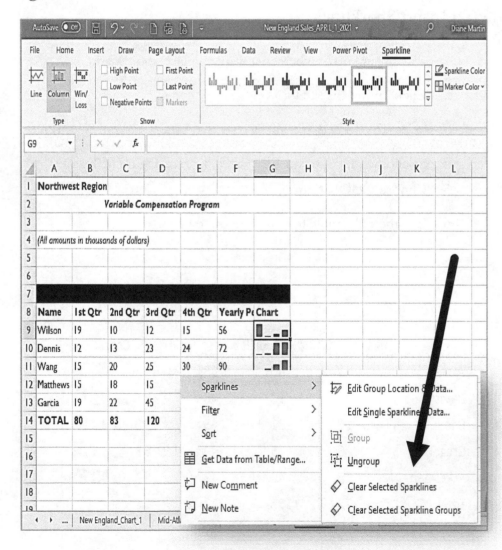

My Notes:

The Power of Tables in MS-Excel

The Tables feature in Excel is designed to facilitate analysis and data management by giving users the ability to extract data based on specific criteria. Imagine how columns of numerical data can be manipulated and sorted based on a specific set of parameters, and you have an idea about the power of the Tables feature. After creating the table below, notice the dropdown boxes next to each heading. These filter buttons will allow you to sort, control, and extract data from the table.

For example, to view values for the sales team consisting of Martin, Garcia, and Blake, you need only click on the Name dropdown box, click Select the (Select All) box, and then select each name. See the results on the next page.

To Create a Table in Excel

1. Select the Insert tab.

2. Choose the Tables button.

3. At the Create Table prompt, choose OK.

Figure 74

	A	B	C	D	E	F
1	Mid-Atlantic Region Management Performance					
2	Variable Compensation Program					
3	(All amounts in thousands of dollars)					
4						
5	Name	1st Qtr	2nd Qtr	3rd Qtr	4th Qtr	Total
6	Redfeather	53	47	85	86	271
7	Martin	52	49	67	90	258
8	Wilson	45	48	63	74	230
9	Blake	45	46	49	49	189
10	Jenkins	44	20	40	40	144
11	Travis	40	26	29	29	124
12	Ceasar	37	39	35	33	144
13	Patel	36	39	81	80	236
14	Garcia	30	42	67	92	231
15	Lee	29	40	66	90	225
16	Mancini	26	40	82	40	188
17	Washingto	25	33	42	52	152
18	Anders	25	23	32	28	108
19	Edwardsor	23	28	32	35	118
20	Ming	20	26	100	32	178
21	Rosen	15	12	35	16	78
22	Rivera	10	25	41	31	107
23						

An Example of a Filtered Table

Filtering is a valuable tool for enabling you to extract and focus on specific data. See Figure 75, and note that by selecting the Name Filter button, we can limit our view of the data to those three employees. To clear your filter, simply select the desired filter button and choose Clear Filter.

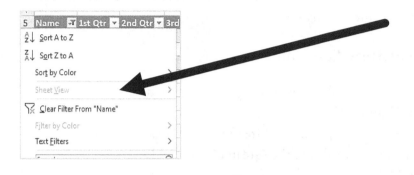

Figure 75

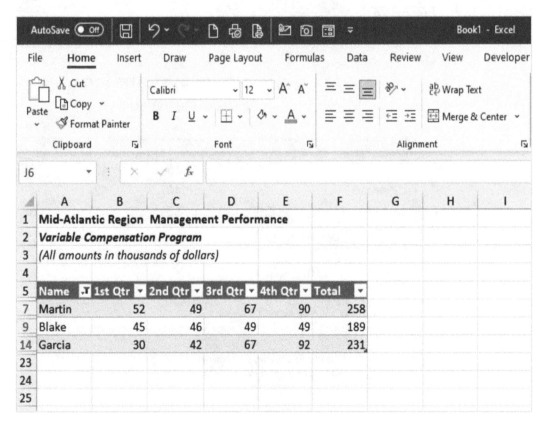

Filtering Data That Meets Specific Criteria

If you are only interested in values above, below, or between a specified value you will find the table feature very useful.

For example, let's say that you are only interested in examining values above 35. In the figure below we are taking advantage of the Custom AutoFilter within Tables to limit our view to those values greater than 35.

To use the Custom AutoFilter

1. Select one of the Filter buttons (representing values)
2. Choose Number Filters.
3. Select the desired option, i.e., Greater Than, Less Than, etc.
4. Enter the desired value in the Greater Than field.
5. Choose OK.

Figure 76

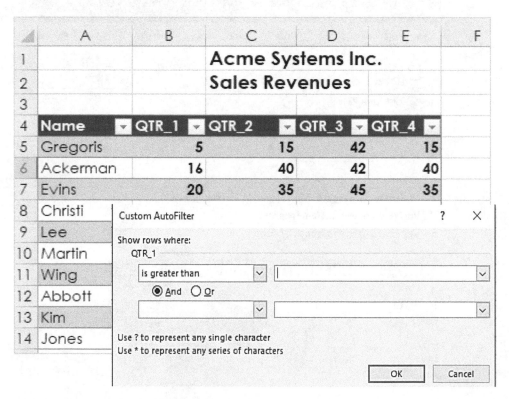

 There is more to learn here. Check out the Numbers and Text filters for more options.

Working with Conditional Formulas

Introduction to the SUMIF Function

While Excel Tables offers the ability to analyze data by filtering, the use of conditional formulas will enable you to filter data by using formulas instead. For example, note that in Figure 77 below there are listed several cities. Supposed you want a formula that will return the sum of any city with a budget below 100 thousand dollars. You might find the SUMIF formula quite useful.

In the result cell (C22), you would type the following: **=SUMIF(C6:C15, "<100")**

As you can see, when entered correctly our formula causes Excel to search the specified range and return the value of $95 for Newtown, as that meets the condition we specified.

Figure 77

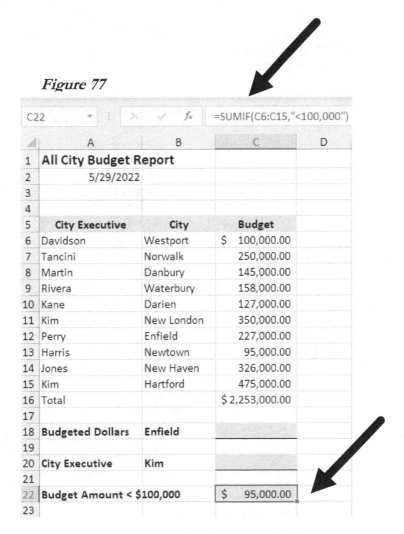

Working with the SUMIF Formula - *continued*

With the SUMIF function, we can also extract data using textual labels. Examine the worksheet below. Suppose you are only interested in viewing the budget of a particular city where Kim is the executive. In that case, you would need to choose your result cell, and then enter the following formula: **=SUMIF(A6:A15, "Kim", C6:C15).** See Figure 78 below.

With this formula, Excel will search the range A6:A15, check for "Kim" and then perform a sum function on any numbers in the range C6:C15 where Kim is the City Executive as that meets the specified condition.

Figure 78

C20		fx	=SUMIF(A6:A15,"Kim",C6:C15)	
	A	B	C	D
1	All City Budget Report			
2	5/29/2022			
3				
4				
5	City Executive	City	Budget	
6	Davidson	Westport	$ 100,000.00	
7	Tancini	Norwalk	250,000.00	
8	Martin	Danbury	145,000.00	
9	Rivera	Waterbury	158,000.00	
10	Kane	Darien	127,000.00	
11	Kim	New London	350,000.00	
12	Perry	Enfield	227,000.00	
13	Harris	Newtown	95,000.00	
14	Jones	New Haven	326,000.00	
15	Kim	Hartford	475,000.00	
16	Total		$ 2,253,000.00	
17				
18	Budgeted Dollars	Enfield		
19				
20	City Executive	Kim	$ 825,000.00	
21				
22	Budget Amount < $100,000		$ 95,000.00	
23				

Don't worry if this function seems a little hard to understand. After you have practiced using the SUMIF function, you will have a better understanding of this powerful function. See the next page for another example of the SUMIF function at work, and then try working through the practice exercise at the end of the book.

The SUMIF Function – *continued*

Here is yet another example of the SUMIF function at work. Let's assume you are only interested in finding the budget for the city of Enfield. In that case, you would enter your formula into your result cell. Here we are using G4. Now, your formula would look like the following: **=SUMIF(B6:B15, "Enfield", C6:C15)**.

Figure 79

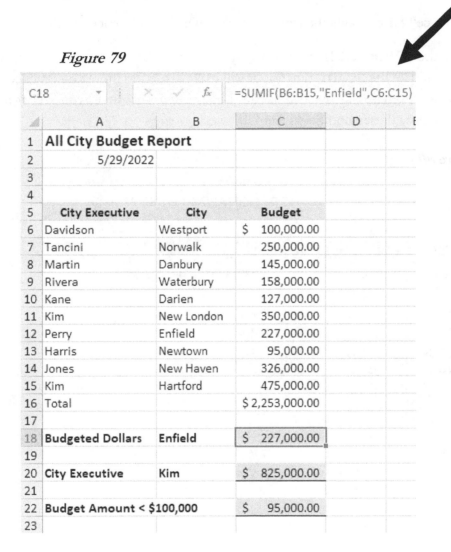

	A	B	C	D	E
	C18		fx	=SUMIF(B6:B15,"Enfield",C6:C15)	
1	All City Budget Report				
2	5/29/2022				
3					
4					
5	City Executive	City	Budget		
6	Davidson	Westport	$ 100,000.00		
7	Tancini	Norwalk	250,000.00		
8	Martin	Danbury	145,000.00		
9	Rivera	Waterbury	158,000.00		
10	Kane	Darien	127,000.00		
11	Kim	New London	350,000.00		
12	Perry	Enfield	227,000.00		
13	Harris	Newtown	95,000.00		
14	Jones	New Haven	326,000.00		
15	Kim	Hartford	475,000.00		
16	Total		$ 2,253,000.00		
17					
18	Budgeted Dollars	Enfield	$ 227,000.00		
19					
20	City Executive	Kim	$ 825,000.00		
21					
22	Budget Amount < $100,000		$ 95,000.00		
23					

 There is more to learn here. Check out other functions like SUMIFS. This function as its name implies gets Excel to add cells that meet multiple criteria. See Online Resources in Appendix C for more information.

Analyzing Data with AVERAGEIF

If you want Excel to calculate the average of a range of numbers if a specific condition exists, the AVERAGEIF function will be useful. Take a look at the example below. Assume that you want Excel to calculate the average of the sales of calendars. Using E2 as the location for our result, we would need to enter the following formula:

=AVERAGEIF(A2:A13, E1, B2:B13).

Note that cell E1 contains the word Calendars which is referenced in the formula.

At first, the AVERAGEIF function may seem counter-intuitive; however, with a little practice and like the SUMIF function it will make sense the more you practice using it. try the practice exercises at the end of the book, and in no time, you will really come to appreciate how these conditional formulas work.

Figure 80

E16		X	✓	f_x	=AVERAGEIF(A2:A13, E1,B2:B13)	

	A	B	C	D	E
1	Goods	Price	Sales Date	Goods	Calendars
2	Stationery	$ 300.00	44635	Calendars Sales Average	
3	Paper	$ 275.00	22-Apr		
4	Pencils	$ 299.00	17-May		
5	Pens	$ 373.00	25-May		
6	Mouse Pads	$ 440.00	14-Feb		
7	Calendars	$ 495.00	27-Feb		
8	Paper Clips	$ 115.00	22-Jan		
9	Pencils	$ 95.00	14-Feb		
10	Tape	$ 156.00	27-Mar		
11	Mouse Pads	$ 300.00	17-May		
12	Calendars	$ 425.00	26-Mar		
13	Tape	$ 148.00	22-Jan		
14					

 There is more to learn here. Try experimenting with the AVERAGEIFS function. Unlike the AVERAGEIF function, the AVERAGEIFS function will calculate the average of cells that meet multiple criteria.

The COUNTIF and COUNTA Functions

The COUNTIF function counts the number of cells in the specified range that contain data matching the specified criteria.

In the example below, I want a formula that counts the number of values that have exceeded the yearly goal. My result cell is D17, and my formula is:

=COUNTIF(G9:G14,">=75").

Note that Excel returns the number 4 in the result cell. In addition to the COUNTIF function, you may also find the COUNTA function useful. For example, suppose I want Excel to count the total number of sales representatives for the East Region. See Figure 82. Here COUNTA returns the value of cells that are not empty. My formula is**=COUNTA(B9:B14)**.

Figure 81

D17 =COUNTIF(G9:G14,">75")

	A	B	C	D	E	F	G
1		**East Region Sales Performance**					
2		***Variable Compensation Program***					
3		*(All amounts in thousands of dollars)*					
4		31-Dec-21					
5							
6							
7							
8		**Name**	**1st Qtr**	**2nd Qtr**	**3rd Qtr**	**4th Qtr**	**Total**
9		Torres	19	20	33	20	92
10		Davis	22	10	20	20	72
11		Chow	10	16	55	16	97
12		Gregoris	5	15	21	21	62
13		Ackerman	16	20	42	20	98
14		Martin	22	32	37	36	127
15		**Total**	94	113	208	133	
16							
17		**Values > $75**		4			
18							

Figure 82

D19 =COUNTA(B9:B14)

	A	B	C	D	E	F	G
1		**East Region Sales Performance**					
2		***Variable Compensation Program***					
3		*(All amounts in thousands of dollars)*					
4		31-Dec-21					
5							
6							
7							
8		**Name**	**1st Qtr**	**2nd Qtr**	**3rd Qtr**	**4th Qtr**	**Total**
9		Torres	19	20	33	20	92
10		Davis	22	10	20	20	72
11		Chow	10	16	55	16	97
12		Gregoris	5	15	21	21	62
13		Ackerman	16	20	42	20	98
14		Martin	22	32	37	36	127
15		**Total**	94	113	208	133	
16							
17		**Values > $75**		4			
18							
19		**No. of Sales Reps**		**6**			
20							

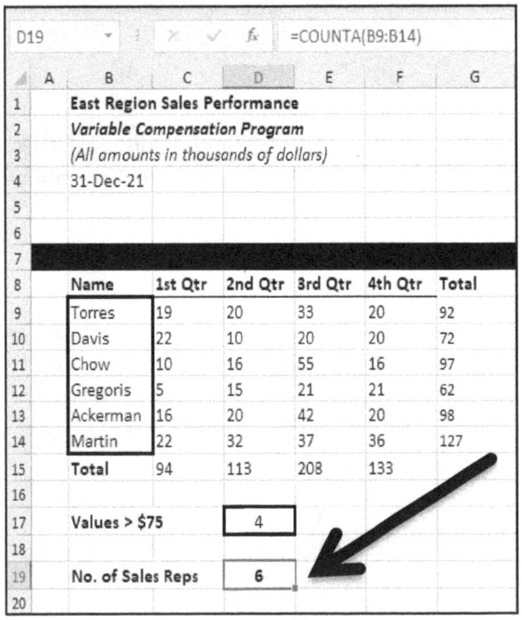

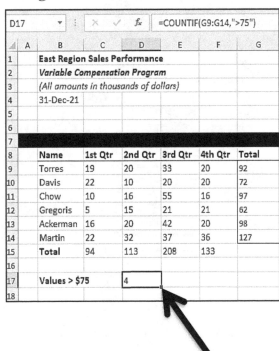

More About the COUNT Functions

Counting things is really what Excel does best and so it should come as no surprise that the COUNT functions are great tools. Whether you need to count money or things, you are sure to find that knowledge of the COUNT functions comes in handy. The COUNT function counts the number of values in a range and ignores all non-numeric characters. In the example below, I am interested in creating a formula that counts the number of orders received. Into my result cell D18, I have entered the formula **=COUNT(C4:C13).**

Figure 83

	A	B	C	D	E
1	Bookstore Order Report				
2					
3	Book #	Author	Order Amount	Vendor #	Payment
4	1200	Chaplin	24	6500	300
5	1201	Brewster	36	3252	443
6	1202	Martin	64	2520	1250
7	1203	Cunningham	40	4625	890
8	1204	Hampton	47	8693	Returned
9	1205	Bell	35	4132	
10	1206	Guzman	45	2580	650
11	1207	Rosales	15	9810	
12	1208	Ganeles	39	3627	4200
13	1209	Wilson	52	4480	7200
14					
15					
16					
17					
18	Total Number of Orders Received			10	
19	Number of Outstanding Orders				

Formula bar: D18 | =COUNT(C4:C13)

There are other COUNT functions, such as COUNTBLANK and COUNTIFS. The COUNTBLANK function for example returns the total number of blank cells in a specified range. See Figure 83 above. To find the number of outstanding payments (represented by blank cells) I would type in D19 the formula =COUNTBLANK(E4:E13).

There is more to learn. The COUNTIFS function works across multiple ranges and counts the number of times all criteria are met. See Online Resources in Appendix C for more information.

Creating Pivot Tables and Charts

An Excel Pivot Table provides a way to isolate view and analyze data in a complex worksheet. Examine Figure 84 below and observe how the three quarters are represented. Assume for example that you have been asked to quickly isolate and display data for just two of the three quarters. The power of Pivot Tables in Excel is that you can among other things, isolate data and limit your report to groups and/or specific elements that meet a stated criterion. See the next page for the steps necessary to create a Pivot Table.

Figure 84

	A	B	C	D	E	F
1	**East Region Sales Report**					
2	*(All amounts in thousands)*					
3						
4						
5	**Name**	**Employee No.**	**Q1**	**Q2**	**Q3**	**Total**
6	Gregoris	100324	5	15	42	62
7	Guzman	100326	16	40	42	98
8	Evins	100328	20	35	45	100
9	Christi	100330	75	62	68	205
10	Lee	100332	78	75	75	228
11	Martin	100334	88	85	95	268
12	Wing	100336	96	88	85	269
13	Abbott	100338	52	65	54	171
14	Bell	100340	16	40	32	88
15	Jones	100342	10	32	55	97
16	Costello	100344	22	15	45	82
17	Smith	100346	19	43	37	99
18	Aspinelli	100348	5	16	43	64
19	Jensen	100350	75	63	67	205
20	Truman	100352	20	35	45	100
21	Washingto	100354	22	32	65	119
22	Harding	100356	19	40	33	92
23	Adams	100358	88	85	85	258

 There is more to learn about Pivot Tables. Explore the Pivot Tables Analyze and Design tabs.

An Example of a Pivot Table at Work

You will find the Pivot Tables feature located within the Tables group on the Insert tab.

To Create a Pivot Table

1. Select the data for your table.
2. Click on the Insert tab.
3. Select the Pivot Table button.
4. Choose From Table or Range.
5. Click OK to accept the default settings. Your Pivot Table will appear on a second worksheet.

After you create your Pivot Table, you can choose the desired view by selecting those fields you wish to see. The Pivot Table Field List will allow you to select the specific fields to be included in your report. See Figure 85 below. Note that the Pivot Table report can also be arranged using the Column Labels, Row Labels, Values, and Report Filter options. You should experiment to find your preferred layout.

Finally, see Figure 86 on the next page and notice that it represents our Pivot Table after Q2, and the Last Name fields have been selected for display.

Figure 85

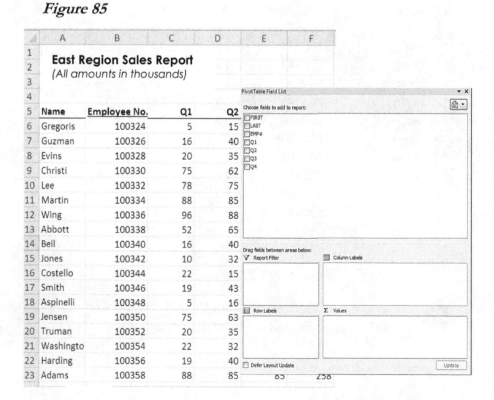

A Pivot Table with Q2 and Name Fields Selected

You will become more comfortable with creating and manipulating Pivot Tables as you experiment with various filters. The Row Labels dropdown box is a good place to start. This is because Pivot Tables will also enable you to filter and sort your data. For example, you can filter results to display values greater than or less than a given number. Alternatively, you can sort table data in ascending or descending order.

Don't be afraid to experiment, because, with Microsoft Excel, you can easily undo your last command. You will find that the multilevel undo command will come in handy as you explore both the Values and Labels filters.

Figure 86

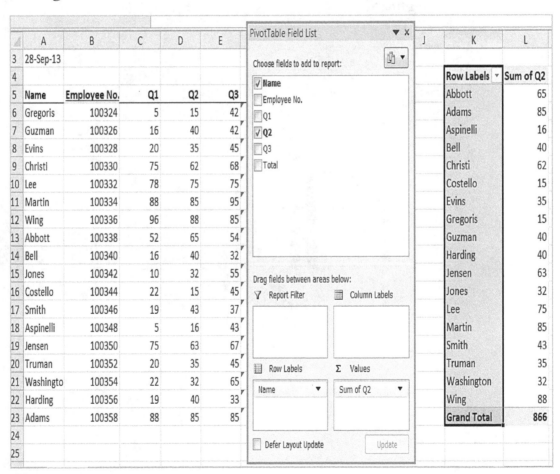

Creating a Pivot Chart

After you create your Pivot Table to isolate a specific set of data, you can graph that data using the Pivot Chart feature. Like the Pivot Table, it will be necessary to first identify the fields to be included in the Pivot Chart. See Figure 87 below. The Pivot Chart now reflects only first and second-quarter results in addition to relevant information such as the name of each of our sales representatives.

The advantage of our Pivot Chart is that now we can expand it if necessary, to include third-quarter results.

Figure 87

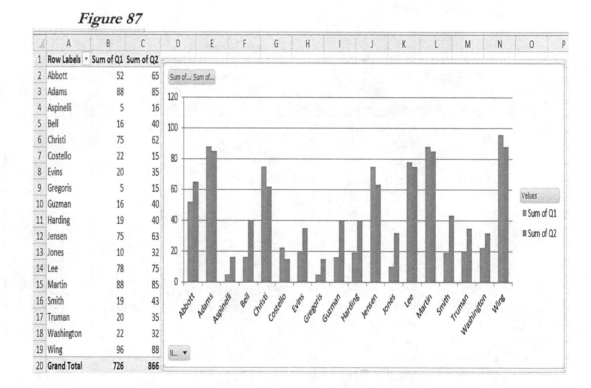

To Create a Pivot Chart

1. Select the range to be included in the chart.

2. Click on the Insert tab.

3. Click on the Pivot Table button.

4. Select Pivot Chart.

5. Type the range to be included in the pivot chart.

6. Click on the fields to be included in the chart (Pivot Table Field List).

Notice that a small button appears in the lower left-hand corner of the chart together with a drop-down box. This button will enable you to filter your data and limit the display to group or individual sales representatives. Click on the dropdown box to view filtering options.

Figure 88

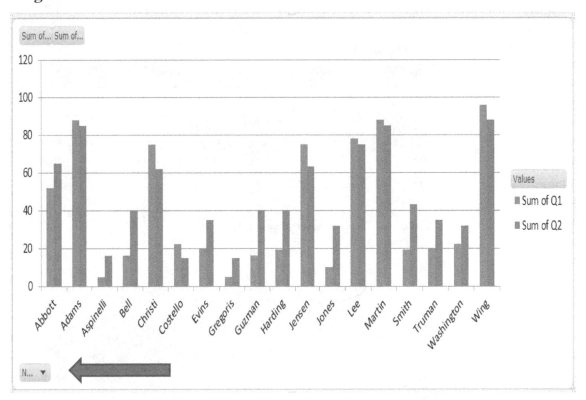

Inserting Slicers

A Slicer is a visual and interactive feature used to filter the data within a Pivot Table. Slicers represent a specific field or set of fields within a Pivot Table. The advantage of creating Slicers is that it makes it easy for others to quickly view a specific subset of your data and they are particularly helpful when users are unfamiliar with how to manipulate Pivot Tables. See Figure 89 and notice that by clicking on Chow's name within the Slicer, I can immediately filter and limit my Pivot Table's display to just her numbers.

The Multiselect button located at the top of the Slicer will enable you to filter more than one field at a time.

The Clear Filter button clears the results and displays all results.

To Create a Slicer

1. Click into the Pivot Table to activate the PivotTable Analyze tab.
2. Click on the Insert Slicer button.

Figure 89

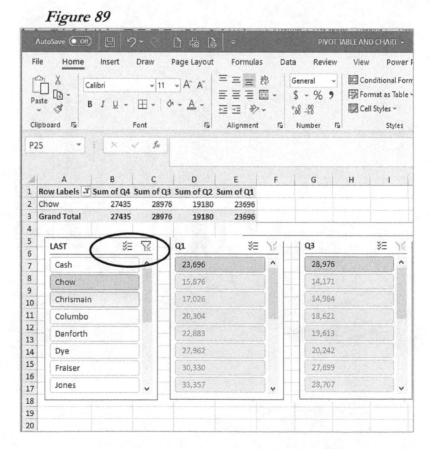

Introduction to Conditional Formatting

As previously discussed, worksheets can become voluminous over time. Therefore, the ability to quickly filter, highlight and/or sort your data can be a real timesaver. Conditional Formatting is an Excel feature that will enable you to highlight trends, values, and patterns within your data by using a combination of color and graphics. For example, suppose I want Excel to highlight in green shading only those representatives who have sold more than $50,000. I can select Conditional Formatting from the Home tab, and then choose the Format cells that are GREATER THAN menu option.

See Figure 90 below and notice that only the cells that meet this condition are highlighted. Note the other built-in Conditional Formatting options such as Less Than, Between, Text that Contains, etc. Additionally, you can create your own Conditional Formatting Rules. See the New Rule menu option.

Figure 90

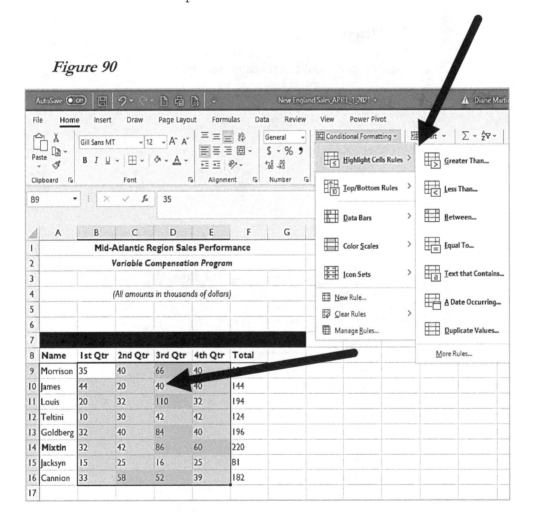

Creating Rules for Conditional Formatting

To Create a New Rule

1. Select the data the new rule will impact.

2. Click on the Conditional Formatting button.

3. Choose the New Rule menu option.

4. Select an option from the Select a Rule Type box.

5. Choose the desired formatting for your rule.

6. Choose OK.

To Delete a Rule

1. Click on the Conditional Formatting button.

2. Choose the Manage Rules menu option.

3. Select the rule you wish to delete.

4. Click the Delete Rule button.

Figure 91

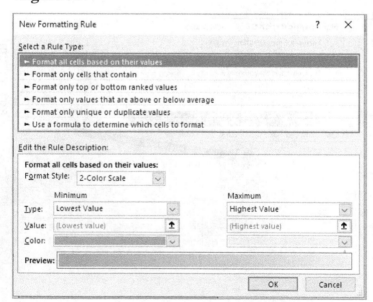

Creating Dashboards in Microsoft Excel 365

A dashboard is a visual representation of key metrics that allow a user to quickly analyze data in one place. Dashboards not only provide consolidated data views but self-service business intelligence opportunity, where users are able to filter the data to display just what is important to them. - Microsoft

Because dashboards have become an increasingly popular tool for analyzing business data, you will want to spend a little time becoming acquainted with its most salient components. The good news is that by now you have probably developed a mastery of those Excel features and functions most often used to create a good working dashboard. Before you embark on the task of creating a dashboard, it will be important to identify your end-users. In other words, you will want to speak with the stakeholders in your organization to be sure you understand how they intend to use the dashboard, and what data or KPI (key performance indicators) will be the most useful to them.

Another important question to consider involves the need to update the data supporting the dashboard. How often will you need to update the data supporting the dashboard? Last but not least, you will need to organize and document the dashboard. See Figure 92 below; this is a sample dashboard. Notice the various components, such as the Table, Charts, Slicers, and Sparklines.

Figure 92

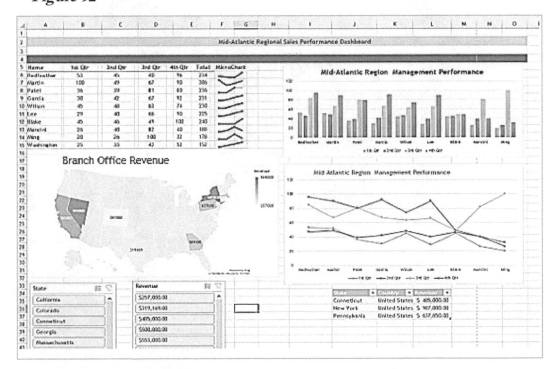

Creating Dashboards in Microsoft Excel 365 -*continued*

The key to creating an effective dashboard is planning. It is highly recommended that you begin by sketching out where data will be placed within the worksheet. I cannot emphasize enough the importance of testing your dashboard. By working with key stakeholders in your organization you can ensure that the time spent putting your dashboard together will be time well spent. You will want to arrange for a small but representative group of employees whose responsibility will be to test the dashboard to ensure it meets the organization's goals and objectives. Collecting information from these end-users will provide you with important information you can use to improve the dashboard. Remember too, the importance of documenting what elements are contained in the dashboard and how each is supposed to work will be key to helping you to maintain and update it.

Figure 93

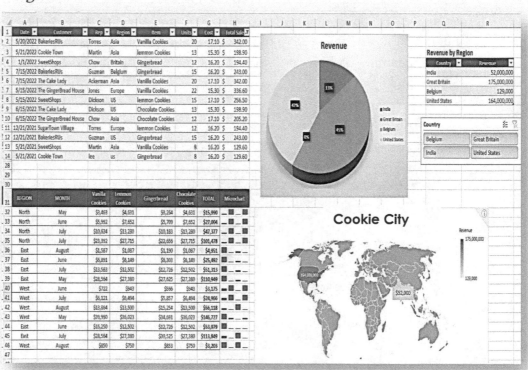

A Sample Dashboard with Table, Map Chart, Pie Chart, And Slicers

My Notes:

Introduction to Date and Time Functions

Worksheets must often include and track financial data as well as other types of information like dates and times. For example, a typical business analyzes its financial performance on a month-to-month as well as a quarterly basis. Often an organization has a critical need to analyze data daily as well. Tracking time-sensitive events like employee time and project management are important objectives. This is why understanding what I refer to collectively as temporal functions in Excel will be extremely useful.

There will likely be times when you come across what appears to be a strange column of numbers purporting to be the date. There is no need to worry; that is just how Excel formats dates. For the application, the date is considered a series. For example, the date 10/21/22 is displayed in Excel as 44855. Of course, you can change the formatting to something more recognizable by selecting the Format Cells feature.

In Chapter 1 you were introduced to two date functions: NOW and TODAY. Recall that with the NOW function, Excel returns the current date and time. In contrast, with the TODAY function, Excel returns just the current date. Other applicable functions include DATE, YEAR, MONTH, DAY, WEEK, MINUTE, SECOND, and NETWORKDAYS to name just a few. In Figure 94 below, I have used the YEAR function in B2 to extract just the year from the date in cell A2. See the table on the next page for examples of other date and time functions.

Figure 94

	A	B	C	D
1	DATE	YEAR	MONTH	DAY
2	Sun, 15-May-22	2022	5	15
3				
4				
5				
6				
7				
8				

Table 1– Date and Time Functions

FUNCTION	EXAMPLE	COMMENTS
=DATE		Combines the values in A2, C2, and B2 to create the completed date.
=MONTH		Extracts the month from a serialized date.
=DAY		Extracts the day of the week from a serialized date.
=HOUR		Returns the hour component of a date/time value.
=MINUTE		Returns the minute component of a time value.
=SECOND		Returns the second component of a date/time value.
=NETWORKDAYS		Returns the number of whole working days between the start date and end date.

DATE and TIME Functions- *continued*

FUNCTION	EXAMPLE	COMMENTS
=TODAY	A2 ▼ X ✓ *fx* =TODAY() ⬜ A | B 1 TODAY'S DATE 2 5/13/2022	Returns the current date
=TODAY()+5	C2 ▼ X ✓ *fx* =TODAY()+5 ⬜ A | B | C 1 Project Start Date | Allocation | Project End Date 2 5/14/2022 | 5 days | 5/19/2022 3	Returns the current date plus 5 days.
NOW	A2 ▼ X ✓ *fx* =NOW() ⬜ A | B 1 TIME NOW 2 Friday, May 13, 2022 @ 03:19:56 PM	Returns the current date and time.
TIME	D2 ▼ X ✓ *fx* =TIME(A2,B2,C2) ⬜ A | B | C | D 1 Hour | Minute | Second | TIME 2 12 | 0 | 0 | 0.50 3 14 | 48 | 10 | 0.62	Creates a time with individual hour, minute, and second components.

As you can see there are several DATE and TIME functions you can use in your Excel formulas. Furthermore, as you become confident with the functions introduced in this chapter, you will discover that these functions can be combined to create very powerful and enduring formulas.

You can begin building your proficiency by doing the DATE and TIME functions practice exercises located in Appendix A.

Calculating with Three-Dimensional References

One of the more fun and interesting features of Microsoft Excel is three-dimensional cell referencing (3-D). This feature actually allows you to construct formulas that calculate your data across multiple worksheets. This can be a real-time-saver where for example, you are looking to create a summary page. The key to using this feature effectively involves setting up your worksheets so that the data you enter appears in the same cells on each worksheet.

The workbook below depicts my summary page. The revenue for each city appears in the other worksheets. My goal will be to construct a formula that will add the total revenue for each branch over the four quarters on my summary page.

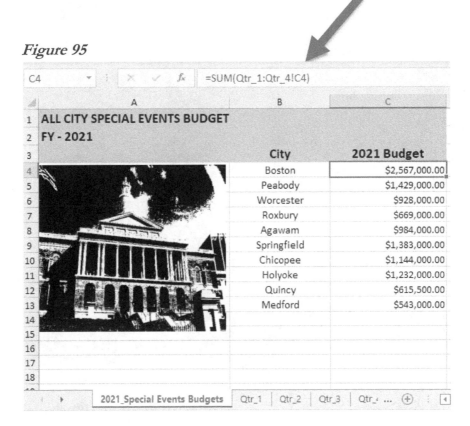

Figure 95

The exclamation point (!) is a delimiter that separates the range in my formula from the target cell. The formula in Figure 95 was constructed by performing the following steps:

1. Click into the result cell (C4) on the summary sheet.
2. Type =Sum(Qtr_1:Qtr_4!C4)
3. Press the Enter key.

Keep in mind that a 3-D reference can include other functions, such as AVERAGE, MAX, MIN, AND COUNT to name just a few.

My Notes:

Automating Tasks with Macros

The Excel Macros feature enables a user to save time by automating certain types of tasks. In effect, Excel allows you to record and store keystrokes and then play them back. For example, suppose that your firm requires that the company name, filename, and current date always appear at the bottom of your spreadsheet. You could just type this information each time you create a new worksheet or, you could record a macro one time and then replay it when needed. The macro will execute all of your keystrokes and save you from having to type the footer information. Before you can create a macro, you will require the use of Excel's Developer Tab.

To Access the Developer Tab

1. Click on the File tab.

2. Click on the Options menu.

3. Select Customize the Ribbon

4. In the Main Tabs list, select the Developer checkbox and then click OK.

The Macros Group

One of the best ways to understand how macros work is to simply record a few of them and then examine exactly how Excel executes its commands.

When you click on the Developer tab, you will see the Code, Add-Ins, Controls, XML, Protect, and Templates groups. These functions enable users to customize the Microsoft Excel environment using several programming features. For now, we will be largely working with the Code group. As you can see, within this group there are five buttons respectively named Visual Basic, Macros, Record Macro, Pause Recording, and Macro Security.

Visual Basic is Microsoft's programming language used in part, to extend the features and functionality of windows-based applications. As discussed previously a macro is a group of keystrokes that can be stored and replayed for the primary purpose of automating otherwise repetitive tasks. These keystrokes can not only be replayed they can be edited within the Visual Basic programming environment. Like most recorders, it is possible to pause recording, thus Excel provides a Pause Recording button. We're now ready to record our first macro.

To Create/Record a New Macro

Goal: Insert the =NOW() command and nsert three (3) new worksheets. See Figure 96 below.

1.   Click on the Developer tab (if not already in view).

2.   Click the Record Macro button.

3.   In the Macro Name box, enter a name for the macro.

4.   Type a letter for the shortcut key.

5.   Select a location for the macro.

6.   Type a description for the macro.

7.   Click OK.

8.   Perform the keystrokes for executing the macro.

9.   Click the Stop Recording button.

Figure 96

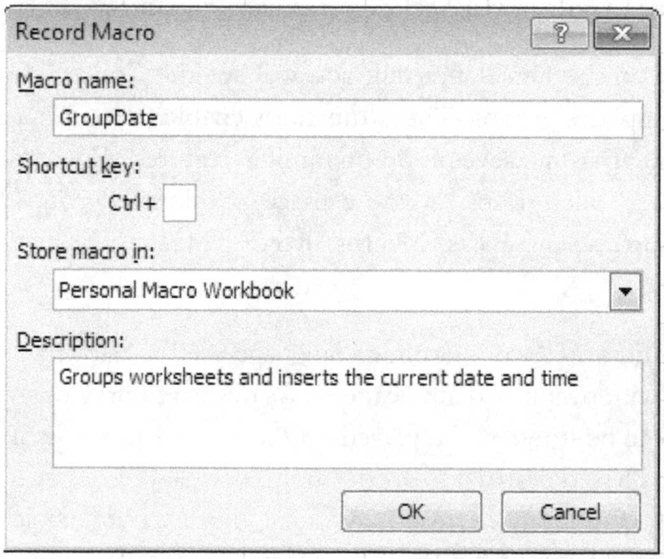

Deleting a Macro

If you no longer wish to keep your Macro, you can delete it simply by selecting the Macros button located on the Developer tab. Moreover, when you have developed proficiency in Excel, you may want to try your hand at editing Macros. An exercise on editing Macros is included in the Practice Exercises in Appendix A.

1. Open the workbook that contains the macro you want to delete.

2. Click on the Developer tab.

3. Click Macros.

4. In the Macros list, select the workbook that contains the macro that you want to delete.

5. In the Macro name box, click the name of the macro that you want to delete.

6. Click Delete.

Figure 97

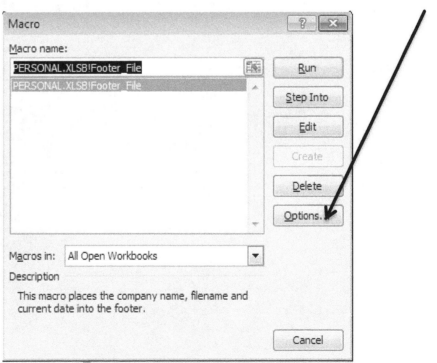

My Notes:

Working with Comments and Notes

Notes

As your worksheets become more complex, and as the need to share them with others becomes important, you will find it increasingly useful to be able to document your data. Fortunately, you can make helpful information available to others by using the Comments and Notes features within Microsoft Excel to accomplish this. For example, to add a simple note to a cell merely select the cell, and then choose Notes from the Review tab. See Figure 98 below and notice the open Notes box. The entire Notes box is editable and can hold more than 3,000 characters.

The Notes box can be closed by selecting the Notes dropdown box and then selecting the Show/Hide Notes menu option. A red dot in the top right corner of the cell will remain a visual indicator that a note is attached to that cell.

To delete a Note, simply right-click on the desired cell, and then select the Delete Note menu option.

Figure 98   *Inserting Notes into a Cell*

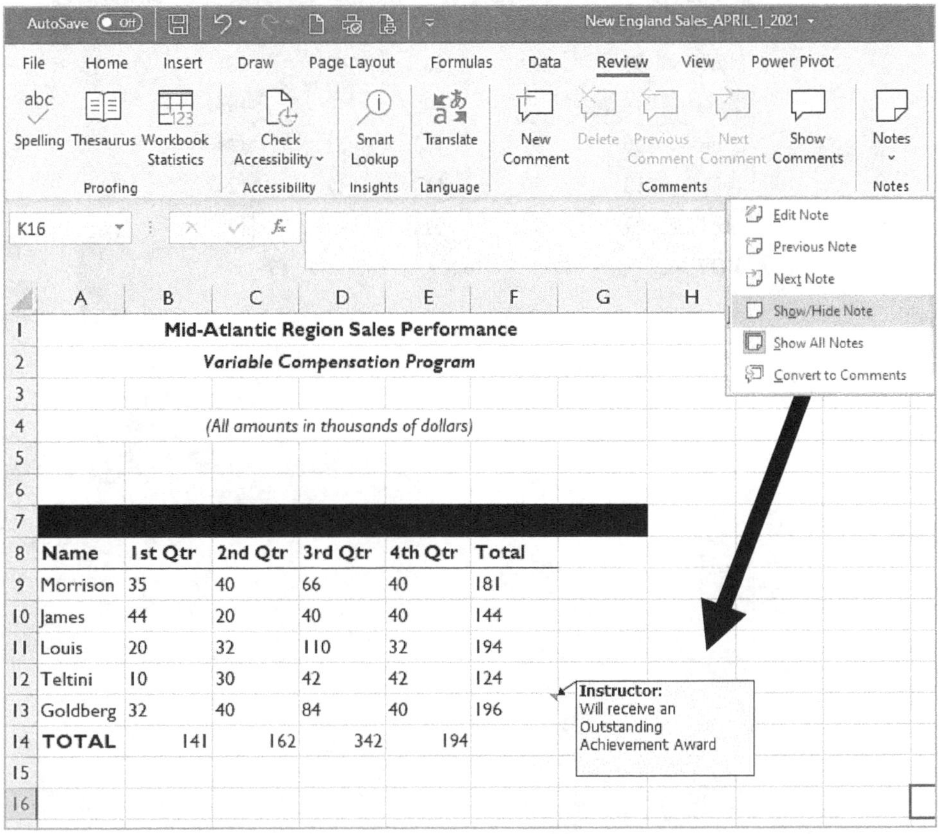

The Comments Feature

Comments are different from notes in that they, (comments) are designed to permit Excel users to enter into a dialog with one another. This feature is particularly geared to users who must share worksheet data. New Microsoft Excel users may not initially require this feature; however, you may likely come across worksheets in which two or more individuals used the Comments feature. Understanding how the feature works will hopefully assist you with understanding the benefits of this pretty cool feature.

In the previous lesson on Notes, you learned that an Excel user can post a note to a particular cell. Others who view the worksheet can simply read the note when they open the worksheet. However, in Figure 99 I have posted instead a comment inquiring about whether a particular employee will receive an achievement award. Because I share my worksheet with my supervisor, he can respond within the same worksheet.

Figure 99   *Comments Lets You Engage in a Dialog*

Name	1st Qtr	2nd Qtr	3rd Qtr	4th Qtr	Total
Morrison	35	40	66	40	181
James	44	20	40	40	144
Louis	20	32	110	32	194
Teltini	10	30	42	42	124
Goldberg	32	40	84	40	196
TOTAL	141	162	342	194	

F13···

When will the Award ceremony happen?

2/14/2021 8:15 AM   Edit

I just learned awards will be given out on May 21.

2/15/2021 3:15 PM

Reply...

Working with Text Functions UPPER AND PROPER

Several practical functions within Microsoft Excel can help you be more productive. This is especially true when you are working with text. As a practical matter, you will likely have to deal with data that is imported into Excel. Unfortunately, it may not be formatted in a way that makes it useful. The good news is that Excel makes several functions available that can help. Notice how in Figure 100 below all of the names in the worksheet are in lower case. This happened because the data was imported from another application. With the help of Excel, lower case names can be converted to initial capitalization using the PROPER function. In contrast, the UPPER function can be used to convert lower case characters to upper case characters. See Figure 101.

Figure 100

	A	B	C	D	E	F
1	cadley	maurice	Cadley	Maurice		
2	davids	Leza				
3	morrow	valerie				
4	adams	evertte				
5	soliz	joanne				
6	martin	diana				
7						

C1 — fx =PROPER(A1:B1)

Check out the formula bar here to see how the UPPER function can be used to convert lower case characters to upper case.

Figure 101

B8 — fx =UPPER(A8)

	A	B	C	D	E
1					
2					
3	Departments				
4					
5	acctng	ACCTNG			
6	tax	TAX			
7	fin	FIN			
8	i/t	I/T			
9					
10					

Using the RIGHT and LEFT Functions

The RIGHT function is used to extract an "n" number of characters from a text string. For example, if you need to export data to another application that only accepts up to six characters for the last name, Excel can aid you in creating a formula that extracts only the six **right-most** characters. See Figure 102 below and notice the argument in the formulas in C4, C6, and C8. Each argument references the specific number of characters to be extracted from the text string.

Hint: Count backward to determine the number of characters.

Figure 102

	A	B	C	D	E	F
1						
2						
3	**Staff Listing**		**TYPE THIS**			**TO GET THIS**
4	Diane Martin		=RIGHT(A4,6)			Martin
5						
6	Michele Hampton		=RIGHT(A6,7)			Hampton
7						
8	Chris Garcia		=RIGHT(A8,6)			Garcia
9						

Like the RIGHT function, the LEFT function is also used to extract an "n" number of characters from a string. In this example, the LEFT function is being used to extract the five **left-most** characters. See our example below.

Figure 103

D4   fx   =LEFT(B4,5)

	A	B	C	D	E	F	G	H	I	J
1	Acme Personnel Listing									
2	First Name	Last Name		Last Name (5 Characters)				Please reduce names for uploading to our database		
3										
4	Dana	Johnson		Johns						
5	Alex	Tremont		Tremo						
6	Lisa	Waking		Wakin						
7	David	Gregoris		Grego						
8	Virgil	Ackerman		Acker						
9	Anna	Markitowitz		Marki						
10	Roberta	Medina		Medin						
11	Kyle	Jackson		Jacks						
12										

Can You Concatenate?

The CONCATENATE function allows you to join or concatenate text strings from multiple cells. For example, suppose you were given a worksheet in which the first and last names of employees are contained within two separate columns. For your purpose, you need the names to be in a single column.

The CONCATENATE function will enable you to "join" the two names so that both appear in a single column. See Figure 104. The quotation marks are used to create the necessary spacing between the two names.

After typing your formula, you can use the Fill Series handle to copy it down.

Figure 104

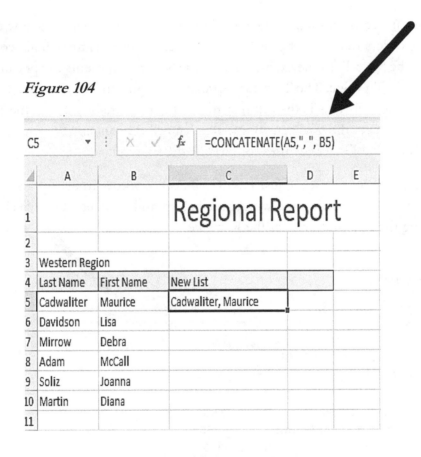

Meet Your Goals with Goal Seek

The Excel Goal Seek feature is a very useful tool for experimenting with values that can generate the desired outcome. The Goal Seek feature is part of the Forecast Group and is located on the Data tab. An example of just how this feature works is depicted in Figure 105 below.

Let's assume that Deana owns a large and successful print shop in town. The building next door has just become vacant, and she wants to expand her business. She will need to borrow $15,000 for the renovations. The average cost of a print job in her shop is approximately $25.00. With Goal Seek Deana can set up a formula that will allow her to see what will happen when she changes one variable like the number of printing orders or units sold.

As you can see from Figure 105, Goal Seek has calculated that Deana will need to fill 600 printing orders to meet her goal. The Goal Seek feature has three main components. First, there is the Set cell. In the example above the Set cell represents the per-unit price. Second, there is the To value. The To value represents the goal in this example. Lastly, there is the By changing cell. This is the cell that represents the variable; that is the number that gets adjusted to meet the goal sought. Notice that cell B3 contains the formula **=B4*B5**. This formula is what Goal Seek uses to calculate the solution.

The best way to appreciate just how Goal Seek works is to set up a scenario like that in Figure 105. Try creating the worksheet below, and then use Goal Seek. Experiment by changing the Per Unit price or the Revenue.

Figure 105

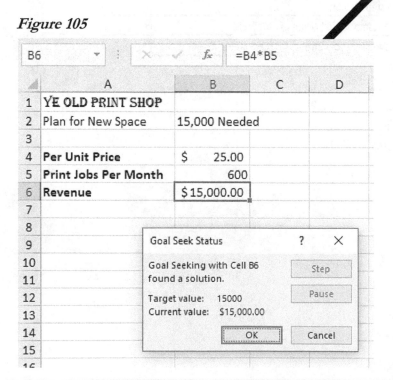

My Notes:

My Notes:

My Notes:

My Notes:

Appendix A

Practice Exercises

Preparing To Practice

Remember what the young man was told when he inquired about how to get to Carnegie Hall; "Practice, practice, practice." In the pages that follow you will find 12 practice exercises designed to help you build your confidence and proficiency in using Microsoft Office. Find a quiet place and time to test yourself on how much you have learned, and do not hesitate to refer to a specific chapter for instructions on how to perform a task. That is the goal of this book.

Note that this book largely covers the basics of Microsoft Excel; however, once you have mastered them you should be ready to tackle some of the more advanced features, and as you can see, an introduction to many of those features is included in this text.

Microsoft Excel Practice Exercise No. 1

This exercise is designed to reinforce what you have learned about, structuring a worksheet, entering data, basic formulas, formatting cells, and saving a workbook. Create the worksheet depicted below. Refer back to Chapters 1 and 3 should you have any difficulty.

1. Create the worksheet depicted below.
2. Construct a formula to calculate monthly sales totals.
3. Construct a formula to calculate quarterly sales totals.
4. Construct a formula to calculate the average monthly sales.
5. Calculate the average for the period January- March.
6. Construct a formula to return the highest and lowest sales amount.
7. Apply bold formatting to the words Marketing Department Report.
8. Apply bold formatting to the words First Quarter.
9. Apply the currency style to worksheet totals.
10. Apply the underline formatting to the months.
11. Save the worksheet as My Marketing Report.

	A	B	C	D	E	F
1		Marketing Department Report				
2		First Quarter				
3						
4						
5						
6	**Account Rep**	**Jan**	**Feb**	**Mar**	**Total**	
7	Guzman	150	350	250		
8	Ewing	200	252	252		
9	Martin	800	300	900		
10	Wilson	900	500	700		
11	Bell	300	370	389		
12	**Total**					
13	**Average**					
14	**High**					
15	**Low**					

Microsoft Excel Practice Exercise No. 2

Basic Formulas and Formatting

1. Create the worksheet below.
2. Use the SUM function to calculate the totals for each month.
3. Use the AVERAGE function to calculate the average number of books sold.
4. Calculate the highest and lowest number of books sold using MAX and MIN.
5. Use the SUM function to calculate the total for the range G5:G14.
6. Apply Bold to the range A4:G4.
7. Right-align text in the range A4:G4.
8. Apply the Center format to the range B5:G13.
9. Apply the Comma style to the range B14:G14.
10. Apply the Underline format to the range B14:G14.
11. Apply the Comma style to the range G5:G15.
12. When you are done, save the worksheet as My Book_Sales_Last_Name.

	A	B	C	D	E	F	G
1			Escribe Publishing Book Sales				5/29/2022
2			Number of Books Sold				
3							
4	**SALES REPS**	**JANUARY**	**FEBRUARY**	**MARCH**	**APRIL**	**MAY**	**TOTAL**
5	Janice Garcia	350	445	450	350	445	2,040
6	Tom Williams	225	650	852	225	650	2,602
7	Patti Agione	650	540	950	650	540	3,330
8	Jane Weathers	557	650	652	557	650	3,066
9	Tammy Goodson	350	445	450	350	445	2,040
10	Chrystal Fields	811	790	980	811	790	4,182
11	Leeza Chow	257	185	236	425	365	1,468
12	Michele Hampton	350	389	388	400	456	1,983
13	Robert Ackers	288	295	299	153	150	1,185
14	TOTAL	3,838	4,389	5,257	3,921	4,491	21,896
15	AVERAGE	426	488	584	436	499	2433
16	HIGH	811	790	980	811	790	4182
17	LOW	225	185	236	153	150	1185

The finished worksheet

Microsoft Excel Practice Exercise No. 3

Creating and Editing Chart Data

1. Open the file My_Book_Sales_Last_Name.
2. Add Bob Kane to the list of Sales Representatives.
3. Select the range A4:F14.
4. Click on the Insert tab.
5. Select the Recommended Charts button.
6. Choose the Clustered Column Chart.
7. Save the file.

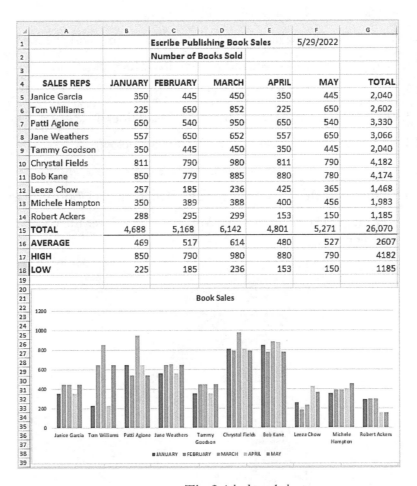

The finished worksheet

Microsoft Excel Practice Exercise No. 4

Inserting Worksheets, SmartArt, Links, and Images

1. Open the file My_Book_Sales_Last_Name.

2. Rename Sheet1 "No. of Books Sold".

3. Insert a new worksheet and name it Book Sales Chart.

4. Move the chart to the Book Sales Chart sheet.

5. Resize the chart so that it extends from the range A2:M30.

6. On the chart, insert an arrow pointing to Chrystal Fields.

7. Apply the Intense Line, Dark 1 theme style to the arrow.

8. In cell D33 type www.escribepublishing.com.

9. Click on the No. of Books Sold worksheet.

10. Insert a stock image of a group of books on the worksheet.

11. Insert a new worksheet and rename it "Infographic".

12. Click on the Insert tab and select SmartArt.

13. From the List category, choose the Basic Block List.

14. Type a month into each block (See image below).

15. Right-click on the Jan block and select Link.

16. In the Type the cell reference field, B14, then click on Infographic.

17. Repeat step 16 for Feb, Mar, Apr, and May- Enter the corresponding cell reference.

18. Save the workbook.

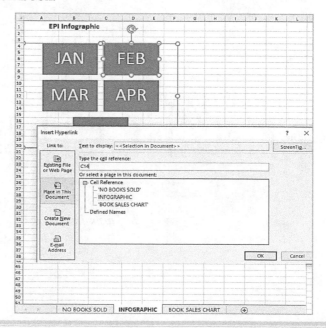

Microsoft Excel Practice Exercise No. 5

Page Layout Features

In this exercise, you will practice what you learned about managing print and page setting options. Do not hesitate to refer to the chapter if you need a refresher.

1. Open the workbook My_Book_Sales_Last_Name.

2. Select the range A1:G30

3. Click on the Page Layout tab and click the Set Print Area button.

4. Click on the File tab.

5. Select the Page Setup link.

6. Change the orientation to landscape.

7. Click on the Margins tab, and change the left and right margins to 1.0

8. Click on the Sheet tab and select the Gridlines checkbox.

9. Save the workbook.

		Escribe Publishing Book Sales				5/29/2022
		Number of Books Sold				
SALES REPS	JANUARY	FEBRUARY	MARCH	APRIL	MAY	TOTAL
Janice Garcia	350	445	450	350	445	2,040
Tom Williams	225	650	852	225	650	2,602
Patti Agione	650	540	950	650	540	3,330
Jane Weathers	557	650	652	557	650	3,066
Tammy Goodson	350	445	450	350	445	2,040
Chrystal Fields	811	790	980	811	790	4,182
Leeza Chow	257	185	236	425	365	1,468
Michele Hampton	350	389	388	400	456	1,983
Robert Ackers	288	295	299	153	150	1,185
TOTAL	3,838	4,389	5,257	3,921	4,491	21,896
AVERAGE	426	488	584	436	499	2433
HIGH	811	790	980	811	790	4182
LOW	225	185	236	153	150	1185

Microsoft Excel Practice Exercise No. 6

Named Ranges and the If Function

In this exercise, you will practice using both Named Ranges and the IF function. Should you need assistance, refer back to Chapter 7.

1. Create the worksheet depicted below.

2. Calculate quarterly and annual totals as shown.

3. Create three Named Ranges: Total, Rate, and Goal.

4. Use the If function to calculate the commission for each representative.

5. Save the file as My Sales Performance Report.

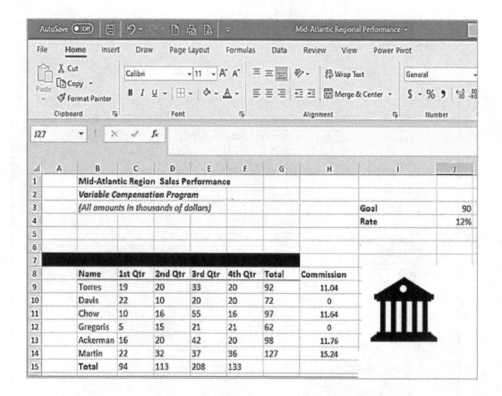

Microsoft Excel Practice Exercise No. 7

Using the VLOOKUP Function

In this exercise, you will work with the file created in Exercise No. 5. Review Chapter 7 to refresh your recollection of Named Ranges and the VLOOKUP function.

1. Open Gradebook.

2. Select the range I3:J6

3. Click into the Name box and name the range Grade_Tbl.

4. Calculate the average for each student in the range G9:G17.

5. Click into the Name box and name the range AVG.

6. Click into cell H9.

7. Select the Formulas tab.

8. Click on the Insert Function button, and then choose VLOOKUP

9. Enter the appropriate range names to calculate the final letter grades.

10. Choose OK, and then use the fill handle to copy the formula down.

11. Save the file as My Gradebook_Last_Name.

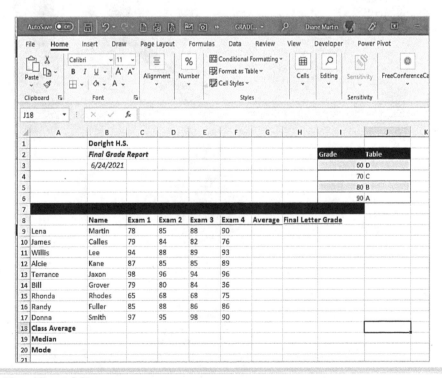

Microsoft Excel Practice Exercise No. 8

Inserting Graphics and Formatting Cells

1. Create the worksheet depicted below and calculate the monthly and annual totals.

2. Apply the currency style as shown below.

3. Apply the Bold formatting style to the Rep, January, February, March, and Total cells.

4. Select and insert an appropriate image into the worksheet.

5. Insert a right-pointing arrow as shown below.

6. Save the workbook as My First Quarter Analysis.

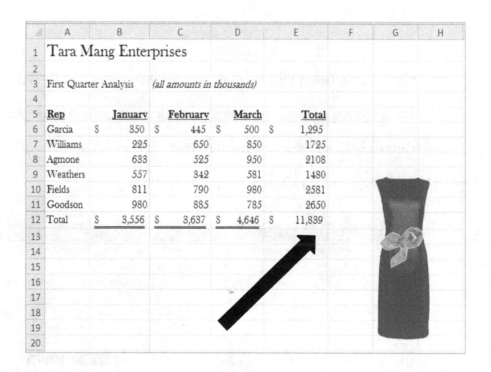

Microsoft Excel Practice Exercise No. 9

More Practice with Inserting Headers and Footers

1. Open the worksheet My First Quarter Analysis depicted below.

2. Insert a header and type Tara Mang Company Confidential.

3. Insert a footer as depicted below.

4. Type the words prepared for the Marketing Department into cell A14.

5. Save the file as My Finished First Quarter Analysis.

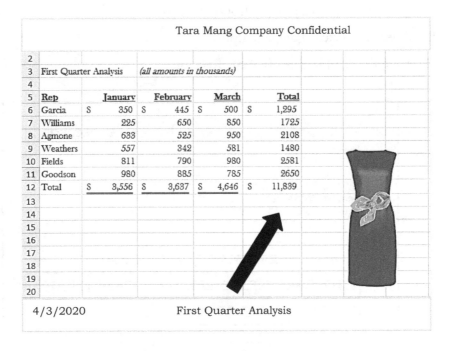

Tara Mang Company Confidential

	Rep	January	February	March	Total		
3	First Quarter Analysis	*(all amounts in thousands)*					
5	**Rep**	**January**	**February**	**March**	**Total**		
6	Garcia	S 350	S 445	S 500	S 1,295		
7	Williams	225	650	850	1725		
8	Agmone	633	525	950	2108		
9	Weathers	557	342	581	1480		
10	Fields	811	790	980	2581		
11	Goodson	980	885	785	2650		
12	Total	S 3,556	S 3,637	S 4,646	S 11,839		

4/3/2020   First Quarter Analysis

Microsoft Excel Practice Exercise No. 10

Editing and Managing Templates

1. Click on the File tab.

2. Select the New menu option.

3. Click into the Search for online templates field.

4. Type receipts.

5. Select the Blue Gradient design sales receipt.

6. Type ABC Publishing Inc. into the company name and address fields.

7. Click on the File tab and choose Save as.

8. Click on the Save as type dropdown box.

9. Select the Excel Template option.

10. Save the template as My ABC Receipt.

Microsoft Excel Practice Exercise No. 11

Applying Conditional Formatting

In this exercise, you will practice applying conditional formatting to the data depicted in the worksheet below.

1. Open Finished First Quarter Analysis.
2. Apply conditional formatting to all values that exceed $500,000 during the period January through March.
3. Create a rule that will highlight all values when they are below $300,000.
4. Test the rule by raising the January numbers for Williams to $350.
5. Save the file.

	Tara Mang Company Confidential					
2						
3	First Quarter Analysis		*(all amounts in thousands)*			
4						
5	**Rep**	**January**	**February**	**March**		**Total**
6	Garcia	S 350	S 445	S 500	S	1,295
7	Williams	225	650	850		1725
8	Agmone	633	525	950		2108
9	Weathers	557	342	581		1480
10	Fields	811	790	980		2581
11	Goodson	980	885	785		2650
12	Total	S 3,556	S 3,637	S 4,646	S	11,839
13						
14						
15						
16						
17						
18						
19						
20						

4/3/2020   First Quarter Analysis

Microsoft Excel Practice Exercise No. 12

Inserting Comments and Notes

In this exercise, you will practice adding notes and comments to a worksheet.

1. Open My First Quarter Analysis.
2. Add the following note to cell A2: *A new goal was set at the last Board of Directors meeting.*
3. Add another note to cell F11 that reads: *The VP wants to give Goodson a bonus.*
4. Assume you share this worksheet with your supervisor. Post the following comment in cell F13: *When will the bonus be awarded?*
5. Save the file as My MidAtlantic_Notes.

			Tara Mang Company Confidential			
2						
3	First Quarter Analysis		*(all amounts in thousands)*			
4						
5	**Rep**		**January**	**February**	**March**	**Total**
6	Garcia	S	350	S 445	S 500	S 1,295
7	Williams		225	650	850	1725
8	Agmone		633	525	950	2108
9	Weathers		557	342	581	1480
10	Fields		811	790	980	2581
11	Goodson		980	885	785	2650
12	Total	S	3,556	S 3,637	S 4,646	S 11,839
13						
14						
15						
16						
17						
18						
19						
20						

4/3/2020   First Quarter Analysis

Microsoft Excel Practice Exercise No. 13

In this exercise, you will record a macro that inserts the current months of the year in Range C6:N6 from the point of the cursor. Name the macro Months. Open a new workbook and run the Months Macro. Use the Ctrl M shortcut key and store it in your Personal Macro Workbook.

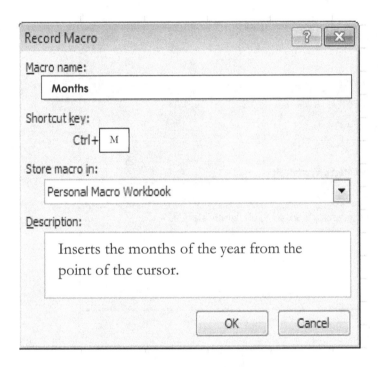

Goal: To record a macro that will create a weekly work schedule- consisting of employee names and days of the week. This worksheet can be used for attendance tracking.

IMPORTANT: Type the employee names in lower case.

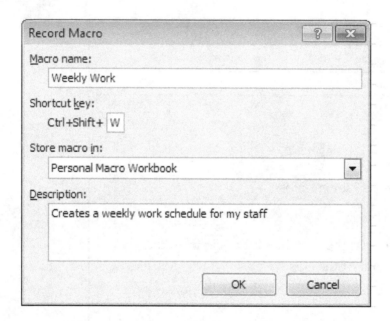

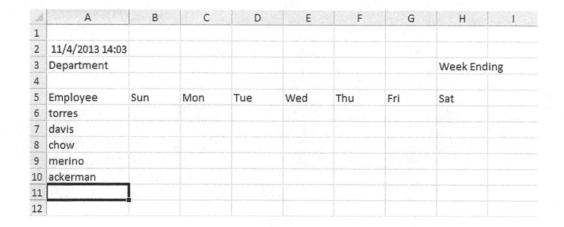

	A	B	C	D	E	F	G	H	I
1									
2	11/4/2013 14:03								
3	Department							Week Ending	
4									
5	Employee	Sun	Mon	Tue	Wed	Thu	Fri	Sat	
6	torres								
7	davis								
8	chow								
9	merino								
10	ackerman								
11									
12									

Microsoft Excel Practice Exercise No. 13 - *continued*

Editing a Macro

1. Click the Macros button.

2. Click the Create button to open the Visual Basic Editor.

3. Edit the macro code

4. Click on the Developer tab.

5. Click the Run button to test the macro.

For Practice: Change the case of the employee's last names within the WeeklyWork Macro

```
(General)                                          ▼   WeeklyWork                                    ▼
        Range("C6").Select
        Selection.AutoFill Destination:=Range("C6:N6"), Type:=xlFillDefault
        Range("C6:N6").Select
        Range("O6").Select
    End Sub
Sub WeeklyWork()
'
' WeeklyWork Macro
' Creates a weekly work schedule for my staff
'
' Keyboard Shortcut: Ctrl+Shift+W
'
        ActiveCell.FormulaR1C1 = "Weekly Work Schedule"
        Range("A3").Select
        ActiveCell.FormulaR1C1 = "Department"
        Range("H3").Select
        ActiveCell.FormulaR1C1 = "Week Ending"
        Range("A5").Select
        ActiveCell.FormulaR1C1 = "Employee"
        Range("B5").Select
        ActiveCell.FormulaR1C1 = "Sun"
        Range("B5").Select
        Selection.AutoFill Destination:=Range("B5:H5"), Type:=xlFillDefault
        Range("B5:H5").Select
        Range("A6:A11").Select
        ActiveCell.FormulaR1C1 = "torres"
        Range("A6:A11").Select
        Range("A7").Activate
        ActiveCell.FormulaR1C1 = "davis"
        Range("A6:A11").Select
        Range("A8").Activate
        ActiveCell.FormulaR1C1 = "chow"
        Range("A6:A11").Select
        Range("A9").Activate
        ActiveCell.FormulaR1C1 = "merino"
        Range("A6:A11").Select
        Range("A10").Activate
        ActiveCell.FormulaR1C1 = "Ackerman"
        Range("A11").Select
    End Sub
```

Microsoft Excel Practice Exercise #14

The Excel Options Menu

In this exercise, you will practice navigating the Excel Options menu.

General Tab

1. Launch Excel 365 and create a new workbook.
2. Select Options from the Backstage view.
3. Set the default number of worksheets to three (3).
4. Select the General tab.
5. Change the default font to Garamond.
6. Change the default font size to 12 pts.

Proofing Tab

1. Make the default view Page Layout.
2. Select the Proofing tab.
3. Choose Autocorrect Options
4. Type your initials in the Replace field.
5. Type your full name in the With field.
6. Click the OK button.

Save Tab

1. Select the Save tab.
2. Set AutoRecover time to every 15 minutes.

Customize the Ribbon and the Quick Access Toolbar

1. Select the Customize the Ribbon tab.
2. Add the Developer tab to the ribbon.
3. Add the Email command to the Quick Access toolbar.
4. Add the Open Recent command to the Quick Access toolbar.

The Advanced Tab

1. Select the Advanced tab.
2. Scroll down to the Display section.
3. Set the value in the Show this number of Recent Workbooks spin box to 12.

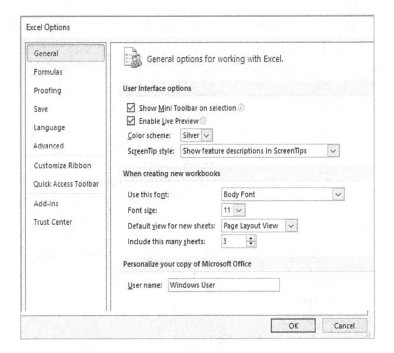

Microsoft Excel Practice Exercise #15

Working with Tables

Open the file New England Table Manners.

1. Sort the sales team's names in alphabetical order.
2. Calculate the total for the range F9:F26.
3. Calculate the average sales for each quarter.
4. Calculate the totals for each quarter.
5. Calculate the highest and lowest values for each quarter.
6. Convert the data to a table.
7. Apply the Light Blue, Table Style Light 16 format.
8. Filter the table to display revenue for Abbott, Harding, and Adams.
9. Save the file as Ne_Table Manners_Your_Last_Name.

	A	B	C	D	E	F
1			**Acme Systems Inc.**			
2			**Sales Revenues**			
3			(All amounts in thousands of dollars)			
4			28-Sep-21			
5						
6						
7						
8	**Name**	**QTR_1**	**QTR_2**	**QTR_3**	**QTR_4**	**Total**
9	Gregoris	5	15	42	15	
10	Ackerman	16	40	42	40	
11	**Evins**	20	35	45	35	
12	Christi	75	62	68	62	
13	Lee	78	75	75	75	
14	Martin	88	85	95	85	
15	Wing	96	88	85	88	
16	Abbott	52	65	54	65	
17	Kim	16	40	32	40	
18	Jones	10	32	55	32	
19	Costello	22	15	45	15	
20	Smith	19	43	37	43	
21	Willes	5	16	43	16	
22	Jensen	75	63	67	63	
23	Truman	20	35	45	35	
24	Washington	22	32	65	32	
25	Harding	19	40	33	40	
26	Adams	88	85	85	85	
27	Total					
28	Average					
29	High					
30	Low					

Microsoft Excel Practice Exercise #16

HLOOKUP Function

1. Open the worksheet: Harry's Hardware.xlsx
2. Construct a formula using HLOOKUP to LOOKUP the number of hammers, screwdrivers, and drills for Day 1, Day 3, and Day 5 as depicted below.
3. Calculate the totals for each product.
4. Display your formulas using the FORMULATEXT function.
5. Save the file as My Harrys Hardware_Last_Name.

	A	B	C	D	E	F	G	H
1	Harry's Hardware							
2								
3		PIPES	CABLES	HAMMERS	SCREWDRIVERS	TACKS	DRILLS	NAILS
4	21-Nov	20	15	16	19	22	25	32
5	22-Nov	15	18	20	22	32	17	16
6	23-Nov	15	14	12	18	22	20	19
7	24-Nov	12	25	28	36	32	30	25
8	25-Nov	26	29	31	30	19	18	16
9	26-Nov	20	15	16	19	22	25	30
10	27-Nov	15	17	22	30	19	29	19
11	Total Week 3							
12								
13		Day 1	Day 2	Day 3	Day 4	Day 5	Day 6	Day 7
14	HAMMERS							
15	SOLD							
16								
17								
18	SCREWDRIVERS							
19								
20	DRILLS							
21								
22								
23								
24								
25								
26								
27								
28								

Microsoft Excel Practice Exercise #17

INDEX and MATCH Function

1. Open the file Acme Quarterly Report_2.

2. Calculate totals for the worksheet.

3. Calculate the average sales for each quarter.

4. Create a formula to return the highest sales for each month.

5. Construct a formula to return the lowest sales for each month.

6. Use the INDEX and MATCH functions to return the first-quarter sales of Caine.

7. Use the INDEX and MATCH functions to return the second-quarter sales of Lane.

8. Use the INDEX AND MATCH functions to return the third quarter sales of Olson.

9. Save the file as My_Index_Match_Last_Name.

	A	B	C	D	E	F	G	H	I
1	Acme Systems Sales Report								
2									
3		Last Name	Quarter 1	Quarter 2	Quarter 3	Quarter 4	Total	Rep	Caine
4	1	Abel	$15,885	$14,625	$6,565	$22,354	$59,429	Qtr_1	
5	2	Caine	$12,500	$5,200	$6,384	$5,500	$29,584		
6	3	Dewey	$11,296	$16,554	$13,867	$25,650	$67,367		
7	4	Casar	$5,752	$6,786	$14,752	$15,850	$43,140	Rep	Lane
8	5	Gaines	$12,699	$7,350	$11,796	$12,600	$44,445	Qtr_2	
9	6	Miranda	$11,652	$8,487	$12,442	$30,525	$63,106		
10	7	Morris	$9,396	$9,589	$8,750	$12,365	$40,100		
11	8	Lane	$7,259	$3,900	$8,845	$10,326	$30,330	Rep	Olson
12	9	Clark	$7,536	$6,183	$3,952	$7,526	$25,197	Qtr_3	
13	10	Olson	11,350	$12,220	$13,500	$15,500	$52,570		
14	11	Cunningham	$8,300	$9,250	$7,580	$12,650	$37,780		
15									

Microsoft Excel Practice Exercise #18

Creating a Dashboard

In this exercise, you will create a dashboard for Acme International's Marketing Department. Your dashboard should resemble the image on Page 115.

1. Open the file Acme International workbook.

2. Rename the first worksheet Mid-Atlantic Sales Data.

3. Add a new worksheet to the Acme International workbook and name it Mid-Atlantic Sales Dashboard.

4. Sort the data in the Mid-Atlantic Sales Datasheet so that those reps with the highest total revenues appear first.

5. Apply Sparklines in the range G8:G24.

6. Graph the data for the range A7:E24 and create a clustered column chart.

7. Move the chart to the Dashboard sheet.

8. Graph the data for the range A7:G24 and create a line chart with markers.

9. Move the chart to the Dashboard and size it appropriately.

10. See the Mid-Atlantic Sales Data Sheet and copy then paste as Link Picture the range that includes the top 10 sales representatives to the Dashboard worksheet.

11. Open the file Acme National Offices and copy the data to the Mid-Atlantic workbook's datasheet and paste the data into cell A35, then create a table.

12. Copy the National Offices table to the dashboard and then create Slicers for each by Quarter and Representative

13. Return to the National Offices table in the datasheet and graph the data as a Filled Map.

14. Copy the Map to the Dashboard.

15. Apply a blue theme to all Acme dashboard elements.

16. Save your file as My_Dashboard_Last_Name.

Microsoft Excel Practice Exercise #19

Pivot Tables, Pivot Charts, and Slicers

Instructions:

1.   Open the file Fourth Quarter Results.
2.   Construct a formula to calculate the totals for each month.
3.   Construct a formula to calculate the average sales for each month.
4.   Calculate the high and lowest numbers for each month.
5.   Insert a Pivot Table.
6.   Isolate quarterly data for Gregoris, Christi, and Garcia.
7.   Apply the currency values for all values.
8.   Create a Name Slicer for the Sales Team.
9.   Graph a Pivot Chart.
10.   Save the file as My PivotTable_Last_Name.

	A	B	C	D	E
3	Fourth Quarter Marketing Report				
4	(All amounts in thousands of dollars)				
5	18-May-22				
6					
7	Name	October	November	December	Total
8	Gregoris	5	15	42	
9	Ackerman	16	40	42	
10	Evans	20	35	45	
11	Christi	75	62	68	
12	Lee	78	75	75	
13	Martin	88	85	95	
14	Wing	96	88	85	
15	Abbott	52	65	54	
16	Kim	16	40	32	
17	Jones	10	32	55	
18	Garcia	22	15	45	
19	Smith	19	43	37	
20	Tinelli	5	16	43	
21	Jensen	75	63	67	
22	Truman	20	35	45	
23	Washington	22	32	65	
24	Harding	19	40	33	
25	Adams	88	85	85	
26	Max	96	88	95	
27	Total				
28	Average				
29	High				
30	Low				

Microsoft Excel Practice Exercise #20

SUMIF and AVERAGEIF Functions

Instructions:

1. Create the worksheet depicted below. Note that all amounts are in thousands.
2. Use the SUMIF function to calculate all cities with revenue above $200,000
3. Use the SUMIF function to calculate the total revenue for Administrator Washington.
4. Use the SUM function to calculate the total of all revenue.
5. Use the SUMIF function to calculate the total revenue for New Haven.
6. Construct a formula using the AVERAGEIF function to calculate the average revenue for all cities generating more than $200,000.
7. Save the file as My_Sumif_Last_Name.

Cities	Administrators	Revenue
Norwalk	Jefferson	200
Danbury	Hamilton	250
Waterbury	Washington	50
Westport	Harris	100
Hartford	Roosevelt	300
New Haven	Kennedy	30
Windsor	Bush	475

Microsoft Excel Practice Exercise #21

COUNT, COUNTA, AND COUNTIF Functions

1. Open the file Count3times.xlsx.

2. Construct formulas to calculate the totals, average and highest sales.

3. Enter a formula using the COUNTA function so Excel counts the total number of employees.

4. Enter a formula using the COUNTIF function to count the number of sales exceeding $50,000

5. Enter a formula to count the number of values in the range E8:E26 that are less than 100.

6. Save the file as My Count3times_Last_Name.

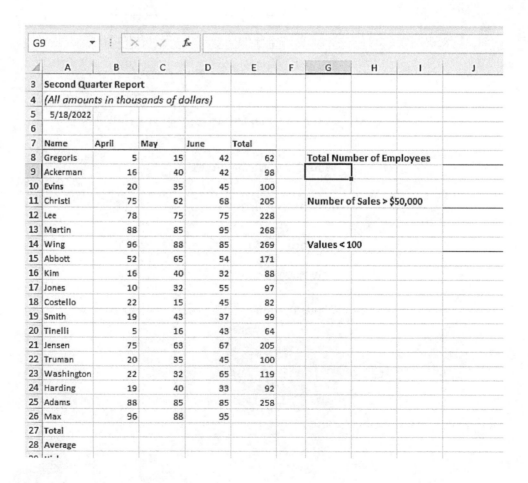

Microsoft Excel Practice Exercise #22

CONCATENATE, UPPER, LOWER, UPPER, and RIGHT Functions

1. Create the worksheet depicted below.
2. Use the CONCATENATE function to merge the employee's last and first names into the third column.
3. Using the LEFT function, construct a formula in Column E that extracts the last five characters from the last name in Column A.
4. Construct a formula In Column G using the LOWER function to reduce all of the names to lower case.
5. Construct a formula in Column I that converts the last names in Column A to upper case.
6. Save the file as My Specialized Functions_Last_Name.

	Last Name	First Name	Joined Names
1	Johnson	Deana	
2	Tremain	Alex	
3	Chow	Lisa	
4	Gregoris	Virgil	
5	Ackerman	David	
6	Martin	Deana	
7	Wells	Orson	
8	Kitty	Carlyle	
9	Marist	Fraiser	
10	Golda	Meyers	
11	Miquel	Garcia	
12	Alan	Lakatini	
13			

Microsoft Excel Practice Exercise #23

Creating 3-D References and Software Integration

1. Open the file Acme National Sales Report
2. Examine each of the worksheets
3. Return to the Sales Summary worksheet.
4. Click your cursor into cell C4
5. Type the formula = SUM(Qtr_1:Qtr_4!C4).
6. Use the Fill handle to copy the formula down.
7. Enter a formula to calculate total branch sales in C17 on the Summary worksheet.
8. Select the range A1:C17 in the Acme Summary worksheet.
9. Right-click on the range and choose Copy.
10. Open the Word file Acme National Sales Memo
11. Paste the worksheet (selecting the Paste Link) option under the heading "Here are the Numbers."
12. Apply the Grid Table Style Colorful, Accent 5.
13. Save the Word file as my National Sales Memo.
14. Save the Excel file as My Acme National Systems Rpt_Last_Name.

	A	B	C
1	Acme Systems Inc		
2	National Sales Report (All Quarters)		
3		Branch Offices	2020-2021 Branch Sales
4		New York	$2,567,000.00
5		Boston	$1,429,000.00
6		Dallas	$928,000.00
7		Philadelphia	$669,000.00
8		Atlanta	$984,000.00
9		Los Angeles	$1,383,000.00
10		Denver	$1,144,000.00
11		San Francisco	$1,232,000.00
12		Newark	$615,500.00
13		Trenton	$543,000.00
14			
15			
16			

Microsoft Excel Practice Exercise #24

Working with Temporal Functions

Instructions: In this exercise, you will reinforce your knowledge of several functions such as DATE, TIME, NOW, TODAY, MONTH, AND NETWORKDAYS.

1. Open the file Temporal Functions.
2. Enter the completed formulas in Column D for each section.
3. Save your file as My Temporal Functions.

	A	B	C	D	E
1	**Date and Time Exercises**				
2					
3	**MONTH**	**DAY**	**YEAR**	**COMPLETED DATE**	
4	3	17	22		
5					
6					
7	**DATE**	**YEAR**	**MONTH**	**DAY**	
8	5/19/2022				
9					
10					
11	**11:30 AM**	**HOUR**			
12					
13					
14					
15	**Project Start Date**	**Project End Date**	**Variance**	**Project Work Days**	
16	12/15/2021	12/28/2021			
17					
18					
19	**Today's Date**				
20					
21	**HOUR**	**MINUTE**	**SECOND**	**TIME**	
22	11	5	0		
23					
24					
25	**Project Start Date**	**Allocation**	**Project End Date**		
26	5/19/2022	13 days			
27					

My Notes:

Appendix C

Common Microsoft Office Keyboard Shortcuts

Ctrl + O	Open an existing worksheet in MS-Office
Ctrl + N	Open a new worksheet
Ctrl + C	Copy the selected data to the Clipboard
Ctrl + X	Delete the selected data- sends it to Clipboard
Ctrl +V	Paste the selected data from the Clipboard
Ctrl + Y	Repeat or redo the last command
Ctrl + P	Executes the Print command
Ctrl + Z	Undo the last command
Ctrl + F	Find (*Word, Excel, PowerPoint*)
Ctrl + R	Replace (*Word, Excel, PowerPoint*)
Ctrl + A	Select All (*Word, Excel, PowerPoint*)
Ctrl + B	Bold text (*Word, Excel, Outlook, PowerPoint*)
Ctrl + U	Underline text (*Word, Excel, Outlook, PowerPoint*)
Ctrl + I	Italicize text (*Word, Excel, Outlook, PowerPoint*)
F1	Execute the Help feature
F7	Execute the Spelling feature

My Notes:

Appendix B - Glossary

_____

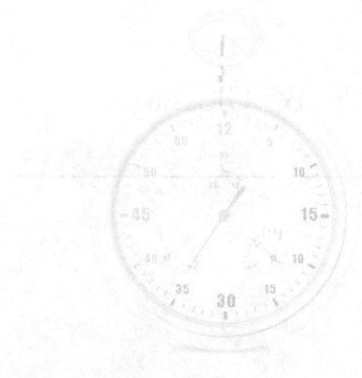

GLOSSARY

Absolute reference: A reference in a formula that does not change when copied.

Accept button: The checkmark button that resides on the formula bar and is used like the enter key to accept the text typed into the active cell.

Active cell: The currently selected cell. A cell must be selected to perform any operation.

AutoSum: An Excel feature that automatically calculates the contents of the selected range based on the selected function, i.e., Sum, Max, Min, Average, etc.

Average function: A built-in function within Excel that returns the average of a range of cells.

Cell: The intersection of a row and a column.

Cancel button: When used before pressing the Enter key, Excel cancels the data within a cell.

Chart: A graphic depiction of a data series. Chart types include bar, column, line, etc.

Footer: Used to place information that is printed in the bottom margin of each page.

Header: Used to place information that is printed in the top margin of each page.

IF function: A function used to construct a logical test in which Excel is required to perform one function if a condition is met and another function if it is not.

Max function: A built-in function within Excel that returns the highest number within a range of cells.

Min function: A built-in function within Excel that returns the lowest number within a range of cells.

Name box: Sits adjacent to the formula bar and is used primarily to create, store and reference named ranges.

Name manager: The Excel feature that facilitates the creation, editing, and deletion of named ranges.

Named range: A group of selected cells that may be referenced by a label as opposed to actual cell references.

Now function: Causes Excel to display the current date and time within the active cell.

GLOSSARY

Fill handle: An Excel feature that facilitates the copying and/or calculation of data across a range of cells.

Pivot Table: An Excel feature that facilitates the visualization, analysis, and summarization of complex data.

Print area: A selected area created for limiting what Excel prints.

Properties: Characteristics about a file that may include the title, file size, creator, date created, file type, and file location.

Quick Analysis: A feature that facilitates the analysis and formatting of data such as charts, tables, formulas, and color-coding.

Range: A selected and rectangular group of adjacent cells.

Relative reference: A cell reference that changes when copied.

Slicers: Used in connection with Pivot Tables to create a visual link to a specific dataset within the table.

Status bar: Appears at the bottom of the worksheet window designed to cue users about the program's readiness to accept commands.

Pivot Chart: A graph based on the data in a Pivot Table.

Sum Function: A built-in function within Excel that sums a range of cells.

Table Array: A range that includes a lookup table.

Tables: A feature that converts a range of cells into a formatted table to facilitate the sorting, filtering, and analysis of data easier.

Templates: A set of pre-designed worksheets that may be customized. Excel comes bundled with dozens of, calendars, planners, invoices, receipts, charts, and budgeting templates.

Themes: A bundled set of colors, fonts, and effects used to give your document a consistent appearance.

Today function: This function causes Excel to display the current date within the active cell.

VLOOKUP function: This function causes Excel to search for the values in the left-most column of a table and then return the value in the same row from a specified column within the table.

Zoom: A feature that enables a user to control the magnification of their worksheet on the screen.

Appendix C

You will find a variety of helpful resources on the World Wide Web; here are just a few examples.

www.microsoft.com

> ➢ Access templates, tutorials, and the latest updates concerning Microsoft Office applications and products.

www.certiport.com

> ➢ Use this portal to obtain information on how to become a certified Microsoft Office Specialist.

www.pcworld.com

> ➢ Keep up to date with the latest software and hardware products on the market.

http://www.pcmag.com/

> ➢ Check out the PC Magazine website for the latest news, downloads, deals, and product reviews.

www.edu.gcfglobal.org

> ➢ A website that provides Online tutorials on Microsoft Office applications.

https://www.customguide.com

> ➢ A good source for Microsoft Excel quick reference cards.

https://exceljet.com

> ➢ Offers Microsoft Office tutorials

Index

INDEX

TODAY function, 5

U

Underline, 3, 23
Undo command, 24
UPPER function, 129

V

Version history, 47
View tab, 55
VLOOKUP function, 79

W

What-If analysis, 132

WordArt, 54

Y

YEAR function, 119

Z

Zoom, 55

My Notes:

My Notes:

About the Author

Diane Martin has been teaching computer applications in the fields of business and higher education since 1981. In 1999, with a background in business and legal technology, she migrated to the field of higher education, becoming an associate dean and program director of computer networking and support for a college of business and technology in New York City. She subsequently taught Computer Applications for Business at LIM College, DeVry Institute of Technology, and the City University of New York. Later she founded My PC Associate NYC a PC training concern. She is the author of several books including "The Manic Manager", Office In a Minute, Steps for Performing Basic Tasks in Microsoft Office 2010/2013" and The Licensing Business Handbook Teacher's Guide" (*EPM Publishing*). Diane is a certified Microsoft Office Specialist. and she is also a certified Senior Professional in Human Resources, (SPHR). She is currently an adjunct professor of business at American International College.

You Can Become an Amazing Manager

The Manic Manager, How to Avoid Becoming the Manager
Everybody Loves to Hate

Available at Amazon.com and other online book retailers

www.escribepublishing.com

My Notes:

Please Let Us Know What You Think

Email your comments to Learner@Escribepublishing.com

Escribe Publishing

Books for the Mind, Heart, and Spirit

My Notes:

My Notes:

My Notes:

My Notes: